From The Women's Press Ltd
124 Shoreditch High Street, London E1

Gillian Perry's interest in Paula Modersohn-Becker comes out of her general interest in and writings on early twentieth century painting in France and Germany and, more specifically, from her work for her doctoral thesis on Paula Modersohn-Becker and the Worpswede artists' colony.

Gillian Perry studied art history at the University of Sussex and now teaches the subject for the Open University. Her home is in London.

Gillian Perry

Paula Modersohn-Becker
Her Life and Work

The Women's Press

First published by The Women's Press Limited 1979
Copyright © Gillian Perry 1979

The Women's Press Limited
A member of the Namara Group
124 Shoreditch High Street, London E1

Typesetting by Clerkenwell Graphics Limited
Origination by Culver Graphics Litho Limited
Printed and bound by Hazell Watson & Viney Limited Aylesbury, Bucks

The Women's Press have also published *Women Artists* by
Karen Petersen & J. J. Wilson, a survey of women's achievement in art
from the early middle ages to the twentieth century. The paperback
edition costs £3.95. If ordering direct please add 30 pence postage & packing.

A complete list of our titles is available. Please send a stamped addressed
envelope with all enquiries.

Contents

Acknowledgements   vi
Biographical Outline   vii

Introduction   1
Paula Modersohn-Becker and Worpswede   13
Images of Women   37
Children   69
Peasants   89
Landscape and Still Life   107
Portraits and Self Portraits   123

List of Illustrations   142
Selected Bibliography   148

Acknowledgements

In this book we have quoted extensively from Modersohn-Becker's letters and diaries which are (as yet) little known outside Germany. The translations are my own, worked on with the help of Christa Broodie-Good, to whom I am deeply indebted.

There are many people to whom I would like to offer my sincere thanks for their cooperation and invaluable assistance in the preparation of this book: the artist's daughter, Fräulein Mathilde Modersohn; Herr Dr Günter Busch of the Kunsthalle Bremen; Herr Wolfgang Werner of the Graphisches Kabinett; Herr Edgar Puvogel of the Ludwig-Roselius Sammlung in the Böttcherstrasse, Bremen; Herr Hans Hermann Rief of the Haus im Schluh Worpswede. I also want to thank John Röhl and Andrew Hardman for their help and criticism, and my publisher, Stephanie Dowrick of The Women's Press, whose interest in Paula Modersohn-Becker made this book possible.

Biographical Outline

1876 Born in Dresden on 8 February, the third of seven children.

1888 Becker family moved to Bremen to a house in the Schwachhauser Heerstrasse.

1892 Took drawing lessons with the Bremen artist Wiegandt. Spent several months with the family of 'Tante Marie' (her father's sister) in London. Attended classes at a London school of art in October.

1893 Persuaded by her parents to begin a two year course in teacher training at the Bremen Lehrerinnenseminar.

1895 Passed her final exams at the Lehrerinnenseminar.

1896 Went to Berlin in the spring. Stayed with Wulff von Bützingslöwen, her uncle, in Schlachtensee, Berlin, and began her studies at the Berlin School of Art for Women. Studied under teachers Dettmann, Stöving, Körte and Haussmann. Impressed by old master paintings (in particular the works of Holbein and Rembrandt) which she saw in the Berlin museum.

1897 Continued her studies at the Berlin School of Art. Joined landscape classes and Jeanne Bauck's portrait classes. Impressed by drawings of Michelangelo and Botticelli which she saw in the Berlin Kupferstichkabinett. Returned to Bremen in the summer. Made her first trip to Worpswede where she took instruction from

Paula Modersohn-Becker, 1902/3

Fritz Mackensen and first met Otto Modersohn. Returned to Berlin in October and participated in the school exhibition. Visited Vienna in November. At the end of the year her father tried unsuccessfully to persuade her to take up a post as a governess.

1898   Studied in Berlin until the summer. Saw an exhibition of works by the Hungarian artist Rippl-Ronai in the Gurlitt gallery. In June and July visited Scandinavia with Wulff von Bützingslöwen. Established herself in Worpswede in the autumn. First met Clara Westhoff.

1899   Spent a week in Berlin in January. Visited Switzerland in the summer. Her work was exhibited publicly for the first time in December in the Bremen Kunsthalle Worpswede exhibition.

1900   Made her first trip to Paris (January to June). Enrolled at the Académie Cola Rossi and visited the anatomy class at the Ecole des Beaux Arts. Spent much time in the Louvre; her letters mention works by Titian, Fra Angelico, Holbein, della Robbia and Donatello. Spent much of her free time with Clara Westhoff who was studying sculpure with Rodin. Met Emil Nolde. Impressed by work of French painters Cottet, Simon, Jean Pierre and Millet. Saw works by Cézanne at Ambroise Vollard's gallery. Modersohn, his wife and Overbeck visited Paris in June. Modersohn's wife died during the visit. After the return to Worpswede Paula became friendly with the poet Rainer Maria Rilke. Announced engagement to Otto Modersohn in late autumn.

With her daughter Mathilde, 1907

1901 Returned to Berlin in January to study cookery in preparation for her marriage. Saw Rilke who was living in the Schmargendorf. Clara came to Berlin in January. Visited Dresden in February. Showed interest in works by Böcklin which she saw in Berlin. Returned to Worpswede in March. Married Otto Modersohn on 25 May. Spent their honeymoon at Carl Hauptmann's house in Schreiberhau. Returned to Worpswede via Prague and Munich.

1903 Made her second visit to Paris (February to March). Returned to the Académie Cola Rossi. Visited a Japanese exhibition with Rilke. Rilke arranged a visit to Rodin's studio and she was impressed with Rodin's watercolours. Sketched from antique and Egyptian works in the Louvre.

1905 Made her third visit to Paris in February. Visited classes at the Académie Julian. Frequently saw her sister Herma who was studying languages in Paris. Saw Rembrandt's engravings in the Bibliothèque Nationale. Visited Cottet's studio and her letters show an interest in the work of Vuillard, Denis and Bonnard. Visited the Salon des Indépendants.

1906 Modersohns stayed with Carl Hauptmann in Schreiberhau in January, travelling back via Berlin where they saw the Centenary Exhibition. She returned to Paris in mid-February, resisting Otto's pleadings to return home. Visited an anatomy class at the Ecole des Beaux Arts. Went with Herma on a trip to Britanny in April. Often visited the Paris studio of the German sculptor Bernhard Hoetger. Sold a still life to Vogeler. Otto came to Paris in June. In the autumn he returned for a longer visit. At the end of the year she exhibited for the second time in Bremen Kunsthalle.

1907 Returned to Worpswede in the early spring. Her pregnancy made it difficult to work during the summer. Gave birth to a daughter on 2 November. Died 21 November of a heart attack.

Introduction

In art one is usually totally alone with oneself.
Paula Modersohn-Becker, Paris, 18 November 1906

On 28 October 1897, at the age of twenty-one, Paula Becker wrote from Berlin:

My whole week has consisted of nothing but work and inspiration. I work with such passion that it shuts out everything else.

Modersohn-Becker's comment illustrates her almost exclusive commitment to art. Between 1900 and her death she found it necessary to spend long periods working in Paris, away from her husband Otto Modersohn and their home in the north German artists' colony of Worpswede. Her final visit to Paris in 1906-7 lasted a year and after several weeks of separation Otto pleaded with her to return home. In her replies to his letters she continually expresses a need to pursue her own separate goals. Working alone in a stimulating Parisian environment she felt that at last she was finding both personal and artistic fulfillment. In a letter of May 1906 to her sister she wrote:

> I am becoming something – I am living the most intensely happy time of my life.

Just over one year later, at the age of thirty-one, Paula Modersohn-Becker died of a heart attack shortly after giving birth to her only child.

Paula Becker was born in Dresden on 8 February 1876, the third of seven children. Her mother came from the aristocratic Bültzings-löwen family and her father, who was born in Russia, the son of an Odessa university lecturer, was an official with the German railway. Her parents created a cultured and intellectual background for their family, frequently inviting writers and artists to their home.

From a very young age Paula showed a talent for drawing and four years after the family had moved to Bremen in 1888, her parents arranged for her to take lessons with a local painter called Wiegandt. In the same year sixteen year old Paula Becker went to stay with relatives in London where she attended art classes which involved drawing from copies of antique statues.[1] In 1893 her parents, aware that art was a difficult and unlikely career for a woman, encouraged her to do a two year teacher-training course in Bremen, hoping that she would then take up a post as a governess. Once she had acquired her teacher's qualifications, which would ensure her employment in the future, her parents agreed somewhat reluctantly to support her studies at the Berlin School of Art for Women.

During her short career Modersohn-Becker's art was hardly known outside Worpswede, although she produced over four hundred paintings and at least one thousand drawings and graphic works. Even her closest friends were unaware of a large amount of her work. Shortly after her death Otto Modersohn and Heinrich Vogeler, another Worpswede artist, visited her studio. In his auto-biography, Vogeler described their reactions:

> It was a great surprise for both of us, even for Otto, to find in the alcoves such a wealth of work – unknown to us . . . We experienced solemn hours here in front of the great works that Paula had left behind.[2]

Modersohn-Becker's personal isolation and her so-called 'valiant

1   *Self Portrait, 1898/9*

struggles'[3] to pursue her art have caused certain misconceptions and oversimplifications of her career as an artist. She was not a misunderstood and diffident 'tragic heroine' who hid herself away in her studio, but a courageous and determined woman. She spent long periods alone in Paris precisely because she had such confidence in her ability and believed that she must pursue her own innovatory style.

She described her own stylistic development as a move towards 'great simplicity of form' (die grösse Einfachheit der Form),[4] but her work fits uneasily into clear cut art historical categories. In general surveys of twentieth century German art she is often referred to as a precursor of the Expressionist movement,[5] although this is an inadequate definition. Later works such as the *Poorhouse Woman with a Glass Bowl*, 1906, or the *Kneeling Mother and Child*, 1907, illustrate a highly individual synthesis of both German and French sources. The rich, thickly applied colours have an expressive quality which could be related to the early Expressionist style of 'die Brücke' group (formed in Dresden in 1905), but her compositions rarely convey the tense restless movement of, for instance, an early die Brücke painting by Ernst Ludwig Kirchner or Emil Nolde.

In both the *Poorhouse Woman with a Glass Bowl* and the *Kneeling Mother and Child* there are strong French influences. By 1906 she had seen works by Gauguin and the Nabis, Maillol, van Gogh and Cézanne, among others. In the *Poorhouse Woman* the crude simplified forms, the emphasis on a two-dimensional schema and the rich colours are reminiscent of Gauguin's syntheticist[6] compositions, many of which were exhibited in his Memorial Exhibition in the Paris Salon d'Automne of 1906. The heavy, almost angular form of the *Kneeling Mother* suggests the influence of both Cézanne's figure studies and the 'primitive' figures of Picasso's pre-Cubist paintings.[7]

However, we do Modersohn-Becker an injustice if we see her only as an eclectic painter whose compositions were derived largely from French post-impressionist sources. Many of her later works, in which she came closest to achieving her 'great simplicity of form', were firmly rooted in the Worpswede environment which was her home. Her favourite subjects, which included work-weary peasants, wistful children and mother and child studies, were often inspired by – or taken directly from – subjects which had attracted her attention within the Worpswede village, and which reflected the aesthetic and iconographical preoccupations of the artists' colony as a whole.

In the autumn of 1898, after completing her studies at the Berlin

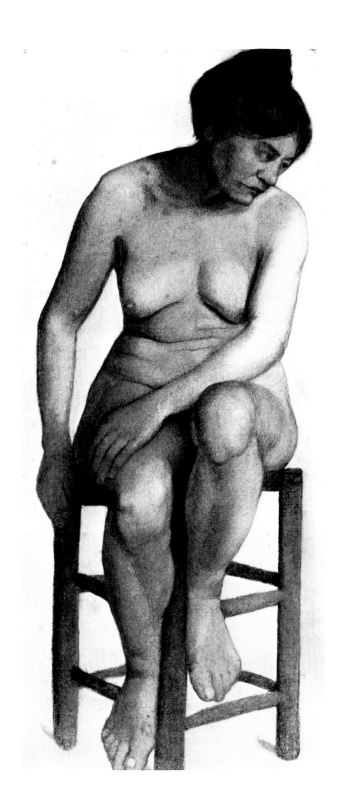

2   *Woman on a Stool, 1899/1900*

School of Art, Paula rented a studio in Worpswede and established herself as a student of Fritz Mackensen, a local artist renowned for his detailed paintings of peasant subjects. She began to involve herself in the social and artistic life of the colony and within the next two years formed several of her closest friendships which were to last for the rest of her life. Here she first met the landscape painter Otto Modersohn (whom she married in 1901), the Jugendstil painter Heinrich Vogeler, the poet Rainer Maria Rilke and Rilke's future wife, the sculptor Clara Westhoff.

In her early landscapes Modersohn-Becker absorbed something of the Worpswede style of semi-impressionist and rather sentimental landscape painting, epitomised in Otto Modersohn's works of the late 1890s and often labelled as 'nature lyricism' (Naturlyrismus). This influence was combined with an intense interest in the local peasant population in which she saw a 'great Biblical simplicity'.[8] For motives which were usually artistic rather than social, she was fascinated with the occupants of the village poorhouse. Here she discovered one of her favourite subjects, an eccentric old woman nicknamed 'Old Dreebeen'.[9] Old Dreebeen was a dwarf whose gross, animal-like proportions lent themselves perfectly to Modersohn-Becker's tendency to monumentalise her compositions. Although influenced by Mackensen in this fascination for local subjects, Paula soon developed in a direction very different from that of her teacher, of whom she wrote in her diary on 1 December 1902:

> Mackensen's way of portraying people is not broad enough, too genre-like for me. If it's possible, one should draw them in runic script.

The 1906 portrait of Old Dreebeen, otherwise known as the *Poorhouse Woman with a Glass Bowl*, is an apt illustration of the way in which Modersohn-Becker came to delineate her subjects in 'runic script'.

Worpswede, like other regionalist artists' colonies which were springing up all over Germany at the turn of the century,[10] was established in a loose spirit of anti-academic revolt. The founder members of the group, Fritz Mackensen, Otto Modersohn and Hans am Ende, who first settled in the village in 1889, were escaping from the artistic restrictions imposed upon them as students of the Düsseldorf and Munich academies. Their gesture was also symptomatic of a broader trend in contemporary German culture to get

II

III

IV

VI

VIII

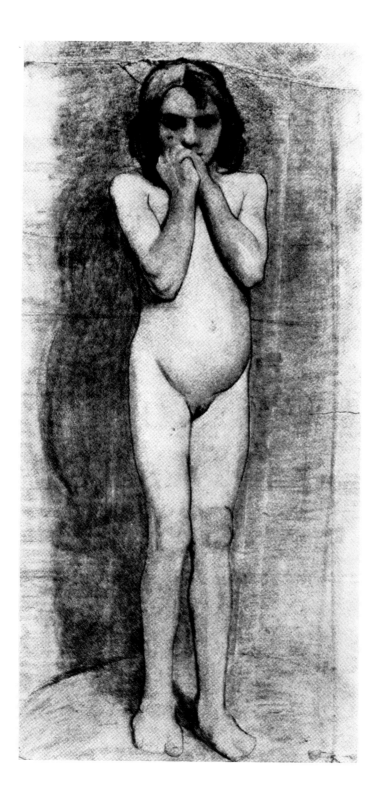

3 *Standing Girl, 1900/1906*

back to one's roots, or 'back to nature'. Through outdoor activities, hikes in the countryside (for which the German Youth Movement became notorious) and a growing interest in local folk culture, young Germans felt that they were searching out the well-springs of their civilisation. It was believed that the virtues of rural life were being eroded by the effects of urbanisation and industrialisation.

These beliefs were nurtured on the writings of popular cultural critics such as Julius Langbehn and Friedrich Nietzsche, both of whom were widely read within the Worpswede circle. Under the influence of Langbehn's book, *Rembrandt as Teacher*,[11] published in 1891, the young artists saw themselves as a close-knit group with a mission to paint their local countryside. In an article in the German art journal, *Die Kunst für Alle* of 1897, the critic Paul Schultze Naumburg wrote that the group was championing a rebirth of art 'through the spirit of the land and its people'.[12]

Although historians have since come to identify this kind of attitude with the seeds of a more ominous right-wing philosophy of 'blood and soil',[13] the original group saw themselves as an idealistic and anti-bourgeois band of artists. Influenced by works like Nietzsche's *Thus Spake Zarathustra* which Modersohn-Becker praises in her diary,[14] they felt themselves to be above the preoccupations of middle class society and its established institutions.

According to her sister Herma, Paula saw herself as a member of a struggling élite.[15] This Nietzschean sense of superiority encouraged Paula in her personal determination to continue painting, despite the general lack of encouragement which she encountered. On 21 September 1899, she wrote from Worpswede to her sister:

> I can see that my aims will diverge more and more from yours. But in spite of this I must follow them. I feel that everyone is frightened of me, yet I must continue further.

At the turn of the century, the environment of an artists' colony provided a relatively tolerant atmosphere in which a woman artist could pursue a career in art. In Worpswede many of Modersohn-Becker's views were reinforced by two other women who were studying art with a view to a career: the sculptor Clara Westhoff and Ottilie Reyländer, another pupil of Fritz Mackensen.

It is, therefore, surprising that in Rilke's monograph on Worpswede, written in 1902 and published one year later,[16] there is no mention of any of the women working in the colony. He was obviously familiar with his wife's work and his diaries show that he

4 *Girl in front of a Window, 1902*

had visited Modersohn-Becker's studio (which he called 'das Lilienatelier').[17] It is possible that Rilke felt that both these women were working in styles which were untypical of the Worpswede nature lyricism which he praises in his monograph. It also seems likely that at the time he did not regard them as serious artists. In a letter of introduction which he wrote on Paula's behalf to the sculptor Rodin (Rilke worked as Rodin's secretary in 1905), he described her as 'the wife of a very well-known German painter'.[18] Paula refers drily to this introductory note in a letter from Paris to Otto in March 1903. She was well aware that as a painter she was generally regarded as inferior to her husband.

Modersohn-Becker's letters and diaries[19] form an intimate and ingenuous testimony to her personal struggles and her commitment to art. She often uses her diaries as a kind of confessional or confidante, as a means of justifying her chosen career to herself and to others. Her need to write a personal diary which combined intimate revelations with a kind of self-encouragement was shared by many women artists, among them her contemporary, the German artist Käthe Kollwitz[20] and the English painter Dora Carrington. Gwen John's 'Notebooks' also include many diary-like entries which are reminiscent of Modersohn-Becker's written comments.[21] In her jottings Gwen John continually emphasises the need for craftsmanship and, like Modersohn-Becker, her commitment to an all-absorbing pursuit of art.

Modersohn-Becker identified many of her own attitudes with those expressed in the diaries of Marie Bashkirtseff,[22] which she read in 1898. Bashkirtseff was a young Russian painter living in Paris who died in 1882 at the age of only twenty-four. Modersohn-Becker's exclamatory style, her attitude to art as the only salvation and her repeated insistence on the necessary loneliness which art entails, are all characteristics which echo Bashkirtseff's diary entries. On the 23 August 1877, the young Russian wrote:

But for art one needs nobody; we depend solely on ourselves . . . Art! I picture it to myself as a great light yonder, very far off; and forgetting everything else, I will walk with my eyes fixed on that light.

Although Modersohn-Becker feared that she did not have Bashkirtseff's strength, she admired her pride and identified with her ambitions. On 15 November 1898 Paula wrote in her own diary:

Her thoughts have got into my blood and they are making me so sad. Like her I find myself saying: When can I really be something!

She was probably referring to Bashkirtseff's comment of 30 September 1878:

I know that I could be somebody, but with petticoats what do you expect one to do? Marriage is the only career for women, men have 36 chances, women have only one.

Notes

1   She describes these classes in letters of 21 and 28 October 1892 from London.

2   H. Vogeler, *Erinnerungen,* Rütten & Loening, Berlin, 1952, pp. 142-3.

3   E. C. Oppler, 'Paula Modersohn-Becker: Some Facts and Legends', *Art Journal,* XXXV/4, 1976, p. 364. In this article Oppler attempts to dispel some of the prevalent myths about Modersohn-Becker's so-called 'tragic' life.

4   Diary entry of 25 February 1903.

5   P. Selz writes: 'Often she is considered one of the significant precursors of the expressionist movement', in *German Expressionist Painting,* Berkeley, 1957, p. 46. And U. Finke writes: 'She successfully managed the transition from nature lyricism to early Expressionism', in *German Painting from Romanticism to Expressionism,* Thames and Hudson, London, 1974, p. 191.

6   'Syntheticism' was a style of painting evolved by Gauguin and Bernard around 1886. It was characterised by simplified forms and suggestive colour, surrounded by dark outlines. It implied a subjective 'synthesis' of the world which would somehow tell 'the truth' about an object.

7   See 'Images of Women'.

8   Diary entry of April 1903.

9   'Dreebeen' was the local dialect for the German word 'dreibeinig', meaning three-legged. The old woman had acquired a three-legged appearance by always leaning helplessly on her stick.

10   Similar colonies were being formed outside large (often industrial) towns all over Germany: Neu Dachau was formed just outside Munich in 1897; Ahrenshoop was formed on the north German coast in 1889; in the 1890s Cronberg was established outside Frankfurt, Grötzingen near Karlsruhe and Cronberg and Dittersbach near Dresden.

11   In an unpublished manuscript of 1938, entitled *Das Weltdorf Worpswede* (Worpswede archives), Mackensen describes how the founder members of the group had 'devoured' Langbehn's book when it first came out. *Rembrandt as Teacher* (*Rembrandt als Erzieher*) was a rather peculiar book in which art and, in particular, the symbol of Rembrandt, was seen as the salvation for a decadent German society. It exalted the German peasant and his 'natural' life-style. The book was so popular that it went into twenty editions in the first year of publication.

12   *Die Kunst für Alle,* XII, 1897, pp. 116-18.

13   G. L. Mosse has attempted to trace the ideological bases of National Socialist ideas in *The Crisis of German Ideology,* Grosset and Dunlap, New York, 1964.

14 Diary entries of 12 December 1898 and of 1900. In the latter she writes: 'With his new values Nietzsche really is a man of gigantic stature.'

15 R. Hetsch, *Paula Modersohn-Becker: Ein Buch der Freundschaft,* Rembrandt, Berlin, p.13.

16 In a letter of 19 February 1903 to Otto, Modersohn-Becker mentions briefly that Rilke's monograph is out.

17 This reference in a letter is cited by H. W. Petzet in *Das Bildnis des Dichters,* Societäts, Frankfurt, 1957, p. 38.

18 *Briefe aus den Jahren 1902-6,* Leipzig, 1930.

19 The many editions of the letters and diaries (Briefe und Tagebuchblätter) which have appeared in Germany since the definitive edition of 1920 indicate their popularity with the German public. The first incomplete edition, *Eine Künstlerin,* appeared in 1917 and 1919, to be followed by an expanded edition in 1920. A popular paperback edition was published by List in 1957, and S. Fischer Verlag have published a new annotated version in 1979.

20 Käthe Kollwitz had also studied at the Berlin School of Art for Women, in 1884.

21 Gwen John's 'Notebooks', as yet unpublished, are in the possession of Mary Taubman. My comments are taken from a paper on the 'Notebooks' which Mary Taubman gave to the Association of Art Historians in Cardiff on 31 March 1978.

22 Translated into English in 1890 by Mathilde Blind. All quotations used in the text are from this edition: *The Journal of Marie Bashkirtseff,* London, 1890.

Paula Modersohn-Becker and Worpswede

In the summer of 1897, while on holiday from the Berlin School of Art for Women, Paula Becker first visited Worpswede. Her earliest impressions of the village are recorded in a diary entry from that summer:

> Worpswede, Worpswede, Worpswede! 'Versunkene Glocke' feeling! Birches, birches, pines and old willows. The beautiful brown moor, delicious brown! The canal boats with their dark sails. It's a wonderland, a land of the Gods. . . .
> . . . Worpswede, Worpswede, you are always on my mind. That was real feeling to the tip of my tiniest finger. Your mighty grandiose pines! I call them my men, broad, gnarled and large, and yet with fine, fine sinews and nerves. I think this is an ideal artistic form. And your birches, the delicate slender young women, which bring joy to the eye.

Her exclamatory style helps to evoke an emotional and idealised vision of Worpswede. She enthuses over the natural motives which

Otto Modersohn, *Autumn in the Moors, 1895*

characterise the local scenery: the moors are not just brown, but a *delicious* brown; the canals are a dark *asphalt* black and the pine and birch trees possess qualities which lead her to personify them as men and women. Like the other early members of the artists' colony, she was looking to nature and the local countryside as a source of artistic inspiration and the 'feeling of a mood' (Stimmungsgefühl). To a certain extent she was seeing nature through the eyes of the Worpswede landscape painters. In their paintings, Otto Modersohn, Fritz Overbeck and Carl Vinnen were all prone to accentuate the powerful forms of the pine trunks, the graceful rhythms of the birch trees or the warm shades of brown to be found in the moors.

The magic of this land seemed to her to parallel the sentiments expressed in Gerhart Hauptmann's *Die Versunkene Glocke* (The Sunken Bell), a romantic novel set in natural surroundings which tells the story of a bell founder who falls in love with an elfin mountain girl.[1] Hauptmann's fairytale, like Paula's first description of Worpswede, creates a remote and unreal world, a 'wonderland'.

Gerhart Hauptmann and Rainer Maria Rilke were two of many writers who were regular visitors to the Worpswede community around 1900. During this period, which has been called 'the era of Worpswede glory',[2] the remote village became a magnet for well-known writers, publishers, art critics, painters and musicians who attended musical evenings held in Heinrich Vogeler's house, the 'Barkenhoff'.[3] Vogeler painted one such evening in a large picture called *Summer Evening at the Barkenhoff*, 1904-5, in which he included

6   Heinrich Vogeler, *Summer Evening at the Barkenhoff, 1904-5*

portraits of (from left to right) Paula Modersohn-Becker, Agnes
Wulff, Otto Modersohn, Clara Rilke-Westhoff, his own wife Martha
Vogeler and the musicians Martin Schröder and Franz Vogeler, with
Heinrich Vogeler himself on the violin.

This environment stimulated many of Modersohn-Becker's own
musical and literary interests. The works of Gerhart Hauptmann and
his brother Carl Hauptmann were well-known in Worpswede, and
there was much discussion of Scandinavian literature by writers such
as Ibsen, Bjornson and Jacobsen.[4] Rilke, who returned from Russia
in 1900, fired Paula's enthusiasm for the works of Tolstoy and
Turgenev.

Worpswede is a small village situated in flat moorland about twenty
miles north of Bremen. In 1889, when the art students Fritz
Mackensen, Hans am Ende and Otto Modersohn established an
artists' colony in the village, the local inhabitants were mostly
farmers and peat cutters. Between 1892-5 the original group was
joined by three more young art students: Heinrich Vogeler, Fritz
Overbeck and Carl Vinnen.

These idealistic young artists felt that they were beginning a new
life. Uninhibited by the constraints of an academic curriculum, they
were free to paint the local countryside. Life in the village also
appealed to them for economic reasons. The cheaper living costs in

the country enticed these art students with limited financial resources. Vogeler has described how initial poverty and difficulties in finding immediate accommodation caused the three founder members to share a tiny room so small that one of the beds had to be placed in front of the door, forcing them to use the window for access.[5]

By the time Paula first visited the colony in 1897 they had established themselves in their own houses and were working in separate studios. Individual artists had begun to sell paintings and make money and Mackensen had set himself up as an art instructor. The group upheld no ideas of communal living; they had no fixed programme and issued no manifesto.[6] The Worpswede artists were a society of friends with similar ideas on art and life, ideas which had been formulated largely during their student days.

Apart from Hans am Ende, an art student from Munich (where he met Mackensen), they had all studied at the Düsseldorf Academy of Art, where the seeds of the colony had been sown in 1885 with the formation of a student fraternity called 'Tartarus'. This group, whose members included all the Düsseldorf students who went on to work in Worpswede, was committed to oppose the rigid teaching methods of the academy. But the positive objectives of Tartarus hardly seem to be revolutionary. They were in favour of a 'respect for nature', selected Old Masters (especially Dürer and Rembrandt) and an ambiguous notion of 'mood' (Stimmung) in painting.[7]

The Düsseldorf Academy, like many German art schools in the late nineteenth century, was, in general, a conservative institution in which students were encouraged to work in officially favoured styles of historical and mythological painting. Imperial authorities and committees with responsibility for the arts in Germany supported a sterile academicism, and in several public speeches and addresses Wilhelm II expressed his disapproval of the modern school of 'Freilichtmalerei' (open-air painting).[8]

This loose art historical term was generally used to describe the works of painters such as Max Liebermann, Lovis Corinth and Fritz von Uhde, who adopted a quasi-impressionistic style. Wilhelm II also disapproved of the subjects preferred by these painters. Like the Worpswede artists, they concentrated on ordinary unsophisticated subjects, instead of heroic or pseudo-classical themes.[9] Liebermann, for example, became notorious for his subjects taken from orphanages and old age homes, themes which are echoed in Modersohn-Becker's works inspired by the inmates of the Worpswede poorhouse.

16

7 *Mother and Child, 1898/9*

8   Worpswede Landscape, 1900

During this period the curriculum in most German art academies was dominated by drawing classes, many of which involved working from plaster copies of original Greek statues. In his autobiography Vogeler has described the frustration felt by many of the Düsseldorf students. He complains about the endless drawing instruction in front of plaster models, questioning the purpose of copying from lifeless objects:

> Through drawing I wanted to feel how a body has grown, not its painterly appearance; I wanted to penetrate its òrganic quality, its structure and its form. Professor Janssen had never come across such a headstrong student.[10]

At the Berlin School of Art for Women Paula Becker also experienced the constraints of the German art education system. Although the Berlin School was sufficiently progressive to have opened its doors to women students (the facilities provided for women were, of course, carefully segregated), the teaching emphasis was primarily on drawing classes. There is no doubt that Paula, who was quite determined to study art, took these classes very seriously, but several of her early letters indicate a desire to work more in oils, a medium in which she so excelled in later works.[11]

On her first visit to Worpswede in 1897 she must have felt that she was among kindred spirits. Here was a group of idealistic artists who, like herself, had chosen to pursue their independent goals in defiance of academic tradition and social pressures. Paula Becker left the Berlin School in 1898 and after a summer trip to Norway she settled in Worpswede. For the time being at least, her parents had agreed to support her and finance her art studies under Fritz Mackensen.

In a broader European context, the Worpswede style of nature lyricism appears to be rather backward looking – reminiscent of the French Barbizon school of atmospheric landscape painting – but in Germany in the 1890s it was seen as a new, even avant-garde type of painting and was often derided by conservative critics. Thus Arthur Fitger, a painter of turgid historical and allegorical works and a bastion of official taste in Bremen,[12] was one of the Worpswede group's most militant opponents. After the first group exhibition in Bremen Kunsthalle in the winter of 1894-5, Fitger used the terms 'Laughter-Room' and 'Apostles of Hate' to describe the Worpswede room and its painters.[13] But public response to this exhibition was

9   Fritz Mackensen, *Prayers on the Moor, 1895*

mixed. After the Bremen show the group was invited to contribute
to the Munich International Glaspalast exhibition of 1895, at which
they met with considerable critical acclaim and Mackensen's painting
of a religious gathering of peasants, *Prayers on the Moor,* 1895,
was awarded a gold medal.

On the occasion of the second Worpswede show in Bremen
Kunsthalle in 1899, in which Paula Becker exhibited publicly for the
first time, Fitger's scorn was still in evidence but this time it was
directed towards the work of the three women painters included in
the show. Apart from several landscapes by Paula, works were
exhibited by Clara Westhoff and Maria Bock, a woman painter who
worked briefly in the colony in 1899 and whose paintings have now
faded into obscurity.[14] Fitger dismissed this group of exhibits as a
demonstration of the 'miserable lack of ability' which one might
expect from 'the naive beginner'.[15]

The group of women artists working in Worpswede around 1900
included Paula Becker, Clara Westhoff, Maria Bock and Ottilie
Reyländer. Paula's letters suggest that they were all close friends who
regularly discussed their ideas on art.[16] Broadly speaking, they
enjoyed more social and artistic freedom in an artists' colony than
they would have experienced within the rigid structure of a segregated art school. In Worpswede they worked and exhibited alongside
the men and generally had their own studios. While working in this

10   Seated Girl, 1898/9

11   *Seated Male Nude, 1898*

12   Spinning Peasant Woman, 1899

environment was not an automatic passport to inclusion in Rilke's monograph, it did provide an atmosphere of relative social tolerance.

Modersohn-Becker spent most of her life from 1898 to 1903 in the colony, working closely with her teacher Mackensen from 1898,[17] and with her husband Otto Modersohn between 1901-3. The instruction which she received from Mackensen is reflected in her series of charcoal, chalk and pencil drawings executed between 1897-1900. These are mostly detailed studies, clearly influenced by her teacher's rigorous insistence on painstaking observation of nature – an attitude inherited from the so-called realist school of German painters.[18] In her diary from the summer of 1897 she expresses a respectful admiration for Mackensen, the painter of 'character-pictures' (Charakterbilder). This term is used to describe his detailed renderings of local peasant types, as is illustrated in the many portrait studies in his *Prayers on the Moor*. The term could be applied equally well to her own drawings such as the *Spinning Peasant Woman* of 1899, the *Seated Girl* of 1899 or the *Seated Male Nude* of 1898. Like her teacher, she frequently shows her subject in profile, carefully delineating an angular or work-weary face.

Even in these early studies her work is evolving beyond Mackensen's doctrine of close observation of nature. She often accentuates physical idiosyncrasies such as a sunken chin, a gnarled hand or a heavily lined face, concentrating on those features which seem to her to express most clearly the subject's personality. This difference in emphasis is the subject of a diary entry of 16 December 1898 when, with a note of irony, she quotes her teacher's views on art:

> Nature should be greater to me than humanity. It speaks louder than I. I should feel small before its greatness. That's what Mackensen wants. That's the alpha and the omega of his teaching. Devoted copying of nature, that's what I should learn. I allow my own little person to step too much into the foreground.

In the first diary entry of 1897 on Worpswede, Paula also praises the landscapes of Otto Modersohn, which she had already seen in the Bremen exhibition of 1894-5. She comments on the powerful sense of mood evoked by his warm autumn landscapes and his sultry evening scenes. This early impression is reinforced in a letter of 9 March 1899 when she sees musical analogies in his use of colour harmonies, and comments: 'Through his paintings he is already so dear to me, a fine dreamer.' Modersohn, the 'fine dreamer' and

12 10 11

13   *The Goosegirl, 1899/1900*

painter of rich musical harmonies, was ideally qualified to inhabit her 'wonderland'.

Modersohn's reactions to the young Paula Becker were no less enthusiastic. In his own diary in 1900 she was the subject of a page of jottings in note form:

1   *Artistic Person*
    purely person[al] ideas on art, painting, literature, (music), enjoyment and creation of art her main objective – and mine.
    Nature, country life, Worpswede, old houses, old establishments etc like me.

2   *Free Person*
    lets herself go regardless. Cheerful, lively fresh temperament. Compensates for mine, that's what I particularly like.

3   Outwardly charming, sweet, strong, healthy, energetic.[19]

Otto and Paula became very close friends after the death of his first wife during a trip to Paris in 1900. He was eleven years her senior and was rapidly winning a reputation in Germany as a talented landscape painter. They became engaged in the autumn of 1900 and the marriage took place on 25 May 1901. Although Paula was clearly in love with Otto, his proposal did present a solution to her current problems. She was still financially dependent on her parents who were exerting fresh pressure on her to become a governess. Marriage would relieve parental obligations, allowing her to continue painting. She also saw in Otto someone who might positively encourage and help her career; as his diary jottings show, they shared many similar ideas on art.

But less than a year after her marriage she began to feel a sense of personal disillusionment. During Easter week, March 1902, she wrote in her diary:

I have cried a lot in my first year of marriage . . . I feel as lonely as I did in my childhood . . . .
It is my experience that marriage does not make one happier. It destroys the illusion that has been the essence of one's previous existence, that there existed something like a soul-mate. The feeling of not being understood is heightened in marriage by the fact that one's entire life beforehand had the aim of finding a being who would understand one. But isn't it better to exist without such an illusion and look this great lonely truth straight in the eye?

14   Children with Geese, 1900

In the two years immediately after the marriage, Paula's personal doubts seem to have been secondary to her preoccupation with her art. She and Otto often worked together on the same subjects. Elsbeth, his young daughter from his first marriage, the garden in Worpswede and characters from the local poorhouse are themes which recur in the works of both artists from this period. There are also strong similarities in style in many of their paintings from 1901-3. The loose, semi-impressionistic brushwork and the two-dimensional quality of Modersohn's portrait, *Paula Modersohn-Becker at her Easel,* 1901, is paralleled in, for example, Modersohn-Becker's *Evening Festival in Worpswede,* 1903.

16

VII

On a purely artistic level, the period spent working closely with her husband in Worpswede was one of mutual encouragement, as is witnessed by an entry in Modersohn's diary on 13 June 1903. He says he is full of hope; while Paula has learnt something from his quality of intimacy, he has been influenced by her free, monumental style. He goes on to comment:

15   Otto Modersohn Sleeping, 1906

She is a genuine artist, of whom there are few in the world, she has something quite rare. Nobody knows her, nobody esteems her. Some day all this will change.[20]

Heinrich Vogeler, another Worpswede figure with whom Paula formed a close friendship, also had some influence on her artistic development. When she established herself in the village in 1898 Vogeler was working on mysterious Jugendstil illustrations and paintings[21]. In her Worpswede diary entry from 1897 she is full of admiration for Vogeler, describing him as a 'charming fellow' who lives in 'his own world'. His illustrations for fairytales and his strange canvases of young girls dreaming under trees, as in *Spring,* 1898, were quite in keeping with what she called her 'Versunkene Glocke' feeling.

17

One of Vogeler's variations on the theme of 'Spring' clearly made an impression on Modersohn-Becker for she discusses it in the same diary entry of 1897, commenting on the way in which the formal precision contributes to an air of serenity and dreaminess. But when she herself later takes up a similar theme, as in the *Trumpeting Girl in*

28

16   Otto Modersohn, *Paula Modersohn-Becker at her Easel, 1901*

17 Heinrich Vogeler, *Spring, 1898*

X *18*

the Birch Wood, 1903, or the *Girl with Cat,* 1905, she discards the realistic style in which Vogeler's mysterious work was 'clothed',[22] thereby also avoiding its sentimental mood. In the *Girl with Cat* the decorative rhythms of the trees, the rough texture of the paint and the simplified forms direct our attention to the formal elements of style rather than the mood evoked by the subject.

Yet despite this difference in emphasis, the vacant stare on the young girl's face is reminiscent of the wistful dreamy expressions of many of Vogeler's subjects, and which can be seen in the portrait of his wife Martha in the centre of the *Barkenhoff.* A similar facial expression appears on the faces of many of Modersohn-Becker's painted children who, like the *Girl in front of a Window,* 1902, stare wistfully out of the canvas.

4

18   *Girl with Cat, 1905*

The fairytale atmosphere and subject matter of many of Vogeler's works had a direct influence on an early Worpswede painting by Modersohn-Becker, the *Teller of Fairytales*, 1900. The strange undulating form of the chairback, the black cat and the mysterious old woman with closed eyes, all suggest a remote and magical world, but a world which has been implanted onto a Worpswede subject.

19   *Teller of Fairytales, 1900*

Many of the letters, diaries and retrospective accounts by members of the Worpswede group single out the regular musical evenings, concerts, gatherings and village dances as the focus of their communal activity. During the musical evenings organised by Vogeler in his 'Barkenhoff', gatherings were held in a candlelit room called the 'White Room'. Both Clara Westhoff and Rilke have described these evenings when Rilke would tell tales of his travels and Vogeler would play his guitar and sing 'nigger songs'.[23] In a diary entry of 1899 Modersohn-Becker describes a similar party at which she was accused of having an insatiable appetite for dancing.[24] Other letters and diary entries indicate that she had a special love for music and dancing, an interest which is reflected in works such as *Trumpeting Girl in the Birch Wood*.

A related theme which preoccupied both Paula and Otto around 1903-4 is the local festival or fair, the subject of her *Evening Festival in Worpswede*. The artificial lighting from the fires and the lanterns, the almost symmetrical rows of women in white festival gowns, and the deliberate elimination of recognisable facial features, give this work a strange eerie quality which is not so far removed from the more overtly mysterious *Teller of Fairytales*.

The themes of the musical evening or the local festival, with their connotations of escapism into the ritual of song, dance and pageant, were an essential part of the separate world which Paula felt she had discovered in Worpswede.

On 16 December 1898 Paula Becker wrote in a letter to her family that she had come to terms with the real meaning of Worpswede. She claims that the 'Versunkene Glocke' feeling which governed her initial reactions was a pleasant dream which could not last. What it really meant for her was a serious struggle to realise her ambitions, to live for art. But throughout her life her professed desire to live for art was inextricably bound up with the belief that this was also a passport to a separate world, a world in which she could find self-fulfillment and independence.[25] During her early career she found this fulfillment by working in the rural surroundings of Worpswede; but around the years 1902-3 she began to yearn for the more stimulating artistic environment of Paris.

The 'great lonely truth' which she acknowledges in her diary in March 1902 encouraged her to spend long periods away from Otto and her domestic commitments in Worpswede: in 1903, 1905 and 1906-7 she made three separate trips to Paris. The first two each lasted several months and the final one over a year. By 1905, her feelings of artistic frustration within the secluded German colony were inseparable from her desire to pursue an independent life. On 13 January 1905, just before leaving for Paris, she wrote to her aunt Marie:

It's strange that from time to time I have a tremendous longing for Paris. It is touching that our life here is built mostly on inner experiences, but sometimes one gets a strong yearning to have an outer life, from which one can always flee if one so wishes.

Worpswede was the source of these 'inner experiences', but not until she was living alone in Paris in 1906 could she write:

I am becoming something – I am living the most intensely happy time of my life.

Notes

1   Gerhart Hauptmann is often described as a naturalist writer in reference to works like his drama *Die Weber* (The Weavers) of 1892, which tells the story of the Silesian workers' revolt. However, by the late 90s he began to write more romantic stories like his *Die Versunkene Glocke*. It tells the story of a bell founder called Heinrich who is split between his love for his wife Magda and an elfin mountain girl called Rautendelein.

2   H. W. Petzet quotes this expression (originally used by Tami Oelkens) in his book *Von Worpswede nach Moskau – Heinrich Vogeler,* Du Mont, Köln, 1972, p. 69.

3   Some of the well-known figures who visited Worpswede included the theatre director Max Rheinhardt, the writers Otto Julius Bierbaum, Richard Dehmel, René Schickele and Carl Hauptmann, the critics Alfred Heymel and Rudolf Alexander Schröder and the composer Paul Scheinpflug.

4   Modersohn-Becker makes several references to both Bjornson and Jacobsen in her letters and diaries. In a letter from Norway of the 3 July 1898 to her family she comments on the fact that Vogeler is illustrating Jacobsen's *Niels Lyhne.*

5   H. Vogeler, *Erinnerungen,* p. 52.

6   Unlike the later German artists' community, die Brücke, formed in Dresden in 1905. Die Brücke artists were staunchly against the traditionalism upheld by the academies and in 1906 issued a short manifesto stating their aims. When the group was first formed they lived communally in a converted butcher's shop in Dresden workers' quarters.

7   An account of the Tartarus fraternity and its objectives can be found in a pamphlet entitled *Karl Krummacher: Worpsweder Maler* (Worpswede Archives).

8   One of Wilhelm's most famous speeches on art was made at the inauguration of the Berlin Siegesallee in 1901. See J. Penzler (ed), *Die Kaiser Wilhelms II in den Jahren 1901 – Ende 1905,* Universal Bibliothek, Leipzig, (no date), p. 57.

9   Corinth did, however, paint several mythological subjects. A notable example is his *Die Kindheit des Zeus* (The Childhood of Zeus) 1905-6, Bremen Kunsthalle.

10   H. Vogeler, *Erinnerungen,* p. 33.

11   See, for instance, her letter of 14 May 1897 from Berlin.

12   For an account of Fitger's life and work as a painter and a poet see G. von Linern, *Arthur Fitger, Maler und Dichter, 1840-1909,* Delmenkorst, 1962.

13   *Kölnische Zeitung,* 1895: see exhibition catalogue *Worpswede: Aus der Frühzeit der Künstlerkolonie,* Bremen, 1970, pp. 51-2.

14 The Bremen Kunsthalle handwritten inventory of works exhibited in the gallery in 1899 includes only four works by Maria Bock: three landscapes and one portrait.

15 *Weser Zeitung,* 20 December 1899.

16 In a letter to her brother, dated June 1899, Modersohn-Becker comments on how well she gets on with Fräulein Westhoff and Frau Bock and how much they are learning from each other. (This letter was first published in 1976 in the exhibition catalogue *Paula Modersohn-Becker: Zeichnungen, Pastelle, Bildentwürfe,* Hamburg, p. 58.)

17 She had also worked briefly with Mackensen during her visit to Worpswede in 1897.

18 Led chiefly by Wilhelm Leibl and Adolf von Menzel, and greatly influenced by Courbet and the French realist school.

19 *Otto Modersohn,* Bremen Kunsthalle exhibition catalogue, 1965, pp. 6-7.

20 Ibid p. 27.

21 In the 1890s Vogeler did, however, paint several landscapes similar in style to those of Otto Modersohn. In his Jugendstil works Vogeler was greatly influenced by the English Pre-Raphaelite painters and by the work of William Morris, Aubrey Beardsley and Walter Crane.

22 Modersohn-Becker uses the word 'kleidet' meaning clothed (Diary, summer, 1897).

23 Clara Westhoff in R. Hetsch, *Ein Buch der Freundschaft,* pp. 45-6. Rilke in *Tagebucher aus der Frühzeit,* Insel, Frankfurt, 1942, p. 277.

24 Letter of 30 March 1899. She describes how Vogeler played and she and Alexander Heymel danced.

25 On 17 December 1897 she wrote to her father: 'Through painting I sometimes transfer myself into my other life.'

Images of Women

The female nude, mother and child groups, adolescent girls and portraits of women are recurring themes in Modersohn-Becker's painted and graphic works. Although she also sketched and painted village boys, farmers and male friends, she was especially pre-occupied with studies of women.

These iconographical preferences were in part determined by the accessibility of subjects and models. Studies from the female nude were a major exercise on the curriculum at the Berlin School of Art for Women, at the Académie Cola Rossi which she attended in Paris in 1900 and 1903, and at the Académie Julian which she visited while in Paris in 1905.[1] In Worpswede most of the local male community was busy working in the fields during the day. Thus, apart from the inmates of the poorhouse, the peasant women and their children were the models most readily available to her in the village.

Modersohn-Becker's work can also be seen as part of a broader pattern of interests of women painters around the turn of the nineteenth century. As in the work of Mary Cassatt, Berthe Morisot or

20 *Self Portrait?, 1897*

Käthe Kollwitz, her iconography often draws upon 'feminine' subjects and experiences of motherhood, although as themes these are not, of course, exclusive to women painters. Linda Nochlin has identified such themes and their various pictorial distillations with a specific socio-historical situation:

> At times when the issues of women's rights, status and identity have been crucial – at present, for example, and in the late 19th and early 20th centuries – this sense of the creative self as woman could play an important role, not merely in choices of subject matter, but in more subtle pictorial variations, as it seems to have done in the work of Paula Modersohn-Becker and Käthe Kollwitz.[2]

These 'more subtle pictorial variations' can be seen in the constant repetition of the self portrait in the work of both Modersohn-Becker and Käthe Kollwitz. Through their many varied interpretations of the theme, both artists reflect a search for their own identities as women. Modersohn-Becker paints herself looking self-assured or wistful, naked or clothed, and sometimes crowned with flowers. She is engaged in a continual process of self-examination.

Unlike Käthe Kollwitz, Modersohn-Becker did not consciously identify her own ambitions or iconographical preferences with the broader issues associated with the Women's Movement at the turn of the century.[3] She saw her struggle to achieve recognition as an artist as a lonely *personal* battle and had mixed feelings about the activities of the German Women's Movement. After attending a lecture in Berlin on 'Goethe and the Emancipation of Women' she praised the speaker (Fräulein von Milde) but found herself unable to agree with the attitudes which 'these modern women' expressed towards men, claiming that the women talk in a manner which portrays men as 'greedy children'.[4]

In some respects, Modersohn-Becker's reservations seem to contradict her enthusiasm for Marie Bashkirtseff's diaries. In her diaries Bashkirtseff dwells increasingly on the limitations imposed upon her as a woman painter,[5] and she began to attend Women's Rights meetings in 1880. Modersohn-Becker, however, saw her own pursuit of a career in art and the collective aims of the Women's Movement as two unrelated issues. According to her sister Herma, 'She always felt herself to be a loner', and was too much involved with her art to expend her energies on the activities of an organisation.[6]

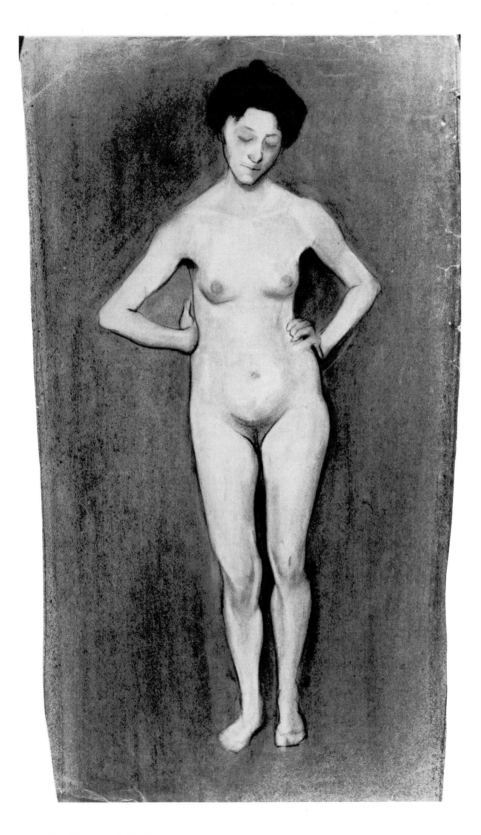

21   Standing Female Nude, c1900

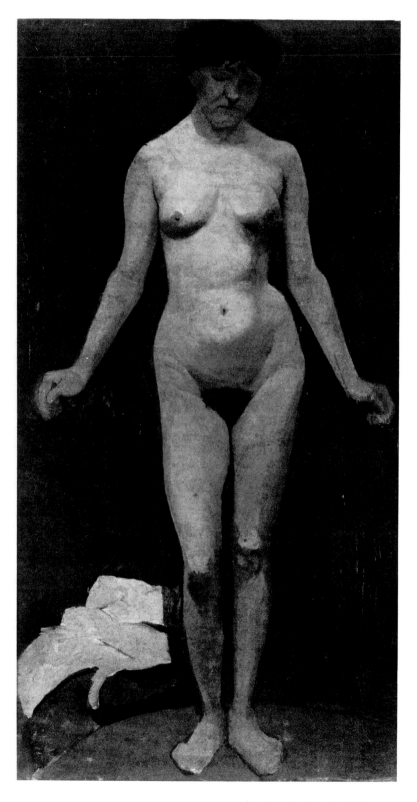

22   *Standing Female Nude, 1900*

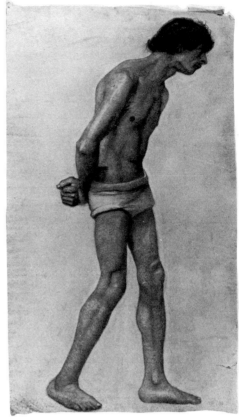

23 *Standing Male Nude, 1896/7*   24 *Male Nude, 1906*

Nude Studies and Life Drawing Classes

23

Modersohn-Becker concentrated her energies on her painting and
her formal art studies. Organised art classes for both men and women
at the turn of the century generally put particular emphasis on the
life drawing class, which formed a large part of Paula Becker's
studies at the Berlin School of Art for Women. Students worked
from nude female models and occasionally (partially clothed!) male
models. Her drawings from these classes are mostly academic
studies in which the models assume traditional poses and the
charcoal medium is used to accentuate contrasts between light and
shadowed areas. This charcoal shading may be used to suggest the
angular lines of an ageing body or the heavy muscular strength of a
male model. Paula's letters and drawings from the Berlin period

indicate that under the influence of various teachers she was experimenting with different styles. While her use of heavy shadows was probably encouraged by her teacher Haussmann,[7] she writes in a letter of 1898 to her father that under the influence of 'Herr A' she is developing a new drawing style in which she takes pains over the contours and outlines.[8]

Both harsh outlines and heavy shadows can be found in her Worpswede nudes from 1898-1900. These works, like many of her early peasant studies, include precise and detailed drawings in which the gradation of tones has an almost photographic quality. Pendulous breasts, pot bellies and heavy awkward bodies are depicted with minute attention to physical peculiarities. Yet these are unselfconscious nude studies in which awkwardness and ugliness have their own special dignity. Gustav Pauli, writing in 1917 in the first catalogue raisonné of Modersohn-Becker's work, found a mysterious

2   25   27

quality of solemnity in these drawings:

> How is it that these early nude studies give the impression of a
> solemnity that is both ceremonious and elevated? They sit there in
> their nakedness, like unveiled mysteries in temples.[9]

The lack of physical idealisation in these solemn works reflects
Paula Becker's concern at the time with anatomical accuracy. In
June 1899 she wrote to her mother that she was working directly
from a skeleton in an attempt to improve her anatomical drawing
and several pages of her sketchbooks from the same year include
sketches of the skeleton and individual bones. The emphasis on
angular bone structure and attention to detail in the 1899 coloured
chalk and charcoal drawing *Nude Girl* suggest that this work was
the result of thorough anatomical study.

Many of Modersohn-Becker's early nude drawings (and peasant
studies) are characterised by lined background shadows. Shaded
areas often consist of linear vertical rhythms suggested by the
charcoal, pencil or brush markings. Günter Busch[10] has compared
this drawing style to the linear emphasis to be found in the work of
Edvard Munch, which she may have come across while in Berlin.[11]

In fact, there seems to be a more direct influence of Munch's work
in her small Berlin sketch of 1898 which has a strong Jugendstil
flavour. The woman's long dark hair, the arms held above the body,
the use of highlights and the evil yet strangely inviting face, are
features reminiscent of Munch's temptresses, in particular his *Madonna*
series.[12] Yet this macabre temptress is untypical of Modersohn-
Becker's work in general and has little in common with the
simplified, primitive female nudes of later Parisian sketches.

Paula Becker's first trip to Paris in 1900 was provoked partly by a
desire to study life drawing at the famous Académie Cola Rossi
which, like the Académie Julian, provided studios for women
students. At the turn of the century Paris was the artistic capital of
Europe, attracting aspiring artists from all over the world. In 1900
the city was also the site of the great World Fair, an enormous
international exhibition of art, design and industrial achievement.
For several months Paris was transformed. The banks of the Seine
were crowded with international pavilions and exhibition halls. On
27 May 1900, standing on the Trocadéro hill and looking down
across Paris, Paula Becker described the city as a scene of 'undreamt-
of profusion'. After the seclusion of Worpswede this environment
seemed indescribably exciting.

II

27

26

26   *Standing Female Nude with Long Hair, 1898*

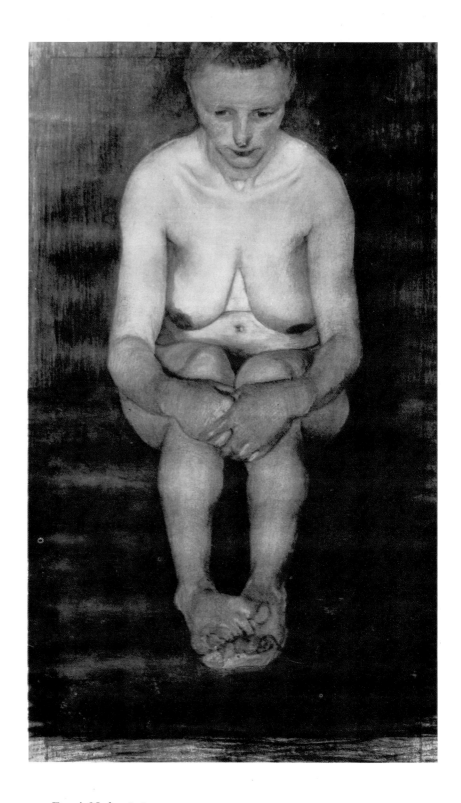

27   *Female Nude, 1898*

28   *Standing Female Nude: Back View, 1906?*

Paula had left for Paris on New Year's Eve 1899. Clara Westhoff, who had encouraged the visit, was waiting for her. Clara had left Worpswede at the end of 1899 to study sculpture with Auguste Rodin. Shortly after her arrival Paula Becker enrolled at the Académie Cola Rossi where she took instruction from three well-known teachers in the French art world: Courtois, Collin and Girandot. In a letter of 18 January 1900 to her father, she describes her week at Cola Rossi's as consisting of life drawing in the morning, followed by a course on quick sketches – called 'croquis' – from the nude in the afternoon. Girandot or Collin would come and correct students' work during the early part of the week, while Courtois, who concentrated on his pupils' use of tones and 'valeurs',[13] would visit the studio towards the end of the week.

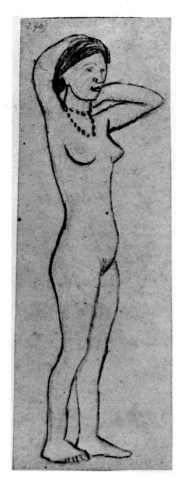

29 *Female Nude with Necklace, 1906*

30 *Two Female Nudes, 1906*

Modersohn-Becker's nude studies from this period reflect the academic poses, often alternating between front and back views, assumed by models in the life class. In their subtle gradations of light and shadow many of these works appear to have been influenced by Courtois's teaching. Even when students at Cola Rossi's were allowed to work in oils, the emphasis on tonal relationships tended to mute the colours. Thus in a letter of 29 January 1900, Paula wrote to Otto Modersohn:

21   22

> At the academy one paints almost without colour. The alpha and omega are the 'valeurs', everything else is secondary.

Modersohn-Becker returned to Cola Rossi's on her second trip to Paris in 1903, although during her third stay in 1905 she enrolled at the Académie Julian, feeling that Cola Rossi's had 'gone to the dogs'.[14]

These two academies, which provided special studios for women, attracted a large number of foreign students around the turn of the nineteenth century. Modersohn-Becker's activities in Paris were typical of many women artists from all over Europe and America who sought to study in the stimulating environment of the French capital. The better known examples include the American artist Mary Cassat who established herself in Paris in the 1870s, studying in the studio of an instructor called Chaplin; Gwen John, who settled in the city in 1903, studying briefly under Whistler and attaching herself to the circle which gathered around Auguste Rodin; and Marie Bashkirtseff and Käthe Kollwitz who both studied at the Académie Julian. Bashkirtseff enrolled in 1877 and Kollwitz attended classes during her visit to Paris in 1904.

The increasing number of enterprising young women students going to Paris to study art inspired an illuminating article in the *Studio* of 1903 in which Clive Holland describes how women artists in the city were 'mostly attached to the classes of the Académie Julian or the Académie Cola Rossi', giving an account of the curriculum in each institution. The article also includes a detailed description of the sort of life which a 'lady art student' could expect to lead in Paris:

> That the life they lead there differs from that led by their male companions, both as regards its freedom and its strenuousness, goes without saying; but it is sufficiently Bohemian for the most enterprising feminine searcher after novelty . . .

31   Lovis Corinth, *Reclining Nude, 1896*

. . . The life of the schools is intensely interesting, often amusing, and sometimes even tragic. The stronger natures among the girl students will probably decide on attending one of the mixed classes, and there they will work shoulder to shoulder with their brother art students, drawing from the costume or the living model in a common spirit of studenthood and camaraderie.[15]

Paula's Parisian trips generally centred around her daily routine at the academy. On each occasion she rented a small room which she also used as her studio, and where she spent much of her time between classes. Holland's report suggests that this sort of life-style in rented accommodation was all too familiar to visiting women artists:

In this little 'appartement' . . . she lives a solitary existence, varied only by the daily visits to the school or atelier to which she has attached herself, the incursions of artist friends (if she be emancipated these will be of both sexes); the occasional visit to a place of amusement, when an escort is available, or the equally occasional dinner at a restaurant.[16]

32 *Reclining Nude, 1905*

In the light of Holland's criteria, Modersohn-Becker appears to have been particularly emancipated. She often saw Rilke while she was in Paris in 1903, 1905 and 1906, and during her last stay she paid regular visits to the German sculptor Bernhard Hoetger. More significantly, in 1900 aged only twenty-four, she courageously visited the studio of the French painter Charles Cottet whose paintings of Breton peasant subjects had caught her attention in the exhibition at the 1900 Paris World Fair.[17] And in a letter of 1905 she wrote to Otto that she wanted to visit the studios of Vuillard and Denis, two French painters whose works, along with those of Bonnard, had particularly impressed her. This determined behaviour was prompted by her belief that one gets 'the strongest impression' in the artist's studio.[18]

The courage and determination which Modersohn-Becker demonstrated in her social and personal life is also reflected in the development of her formal style. While in Paris in 1903 she wrote to Otto that she was evolving a new style. After seeing Rembrandt's paintings in the Louvre she comments that although they are yellow with age they have a rough 'coarse grained' texture also found in old marble and sandstone statuary, and from which she has much to learn. She writes in her diary on 20 February 1903:

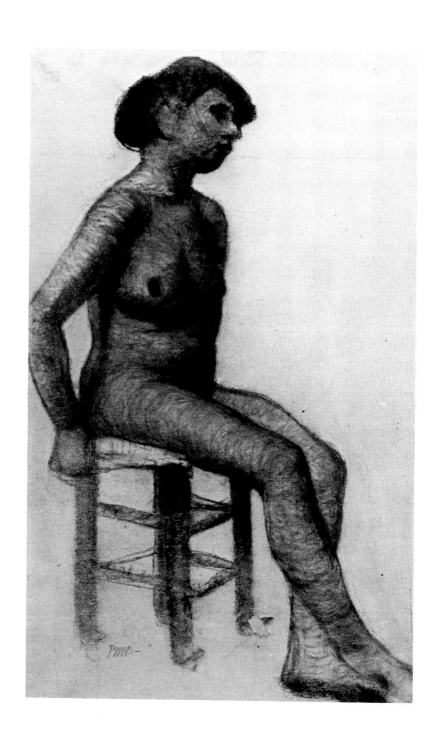

33   Seated Female Nude, 1906

I must learn to express the gentle vibration of things: the intrin-
sically rough texture. I must also find this expression in drawings;
in the way in which I draw my nudes here in Paris, more original
and at the same time sensitively observed.

The rough texture which she describes becomes increasingly
important in her works from around 1903 onwards. In many of her
later paintings the paint surface has a crude unfinished appearance, *40*
showing visible traces of brushmarks.

As is suggested in the quotation above, Modersohn-Becker was
working to achieve this coarse quality, combined with her 'simplicity
of form', in her drawings from the nude. While some of the Parisian
life drawings echo the detailed anatomical accuracy and academic *28*
poses of her Berlin studies, many of the later croquis employ simple
outlines or loose contours which, like her 'runic script' in painting, *30* *33*
have absorbed much from the antique, gothic and Egyptian works
which she saw in the Louvre.[19] On 25 February 1903 she recorded
in her diary:

Up till now the works of antiquity were foreign to me. I could
already find them beautiful, and beautiful in themselves: but I
could find no link between them and modern art. And now I have
found it, and that I believe is progress. I feel there is an inner
relationship from the works of the ancients through to the gothic,
especially the early antique, and from the gothic to my sense of
form.

Great simplicity of form, that is something wonderful.

Modersohn-Becker found a related quality in Rodin's watercolour
drawings, which she saw in his studio in Meudon in 1903, and in
Japanese prints which she saw in an exhibition in February of the
same year. Both these types of work seemed to her to employ a
simple direct style which did not always comply with academic
drawing conventions.[20] Rodin's series of watercolours of Cambodian
dancers (inspired by two visits to Paris by the Cambodian dance
troupe in 1900 and 1906) may have influenced some of her own later
drawings. The loose, summary calligraphy of, for instance, her
sketch *Two Female Nudes*, 1906, is similar to the drawing style of *30*
several of Rodin's sketches of dancers from 1906.[21]

Several letters written during her Parisian trips indicate a profound
admiration for Rodin's work as a whole. In 1900 she praises his
exhibition of sculpture in the Paris World Fair, commenting:

53

He has captured life and the inner spirit of life with tremendous power. For me he can only be compared with Michelangelo, and at the same time he is closer to me in some aspects.

A central theme in Rodin's sculptures, as in many of his drawings, is the naked human body. According to Rilke: 'There was not one part of the human body that was unimportant to him: it was alive.'[22] To the French sculptor every part of the body was a living expression of the character of its subject. His ideas must have featured often in conversations between Modersohn-Becker, Clara Westhoff (who studied at his school in 1900) and Rilke (who worked as his secretary in 1905).

Although Paula did not share Rodin's concern with the expression of bodily movement, she did attach a similar symbolic importance to the naked human body, an importance which went beyond her academic interest in accurate anatomical representation. In a letter of 18 February 1903 to Otto, she compares her own naked body to the idea of her soul laid bare – her nakedness becomes a metaphor for honesty or openness.[23]

XXI
XIV
34

A fascination with her own naked body is illustrated in her many nude self portraits, such as the *Self Portrait with Amber Necklace*, 1906, the *Self Portrait on her Sixth Wedding Day*, 1906, or the now destroyed *Figure Composition*, 1907. The half-draped pose and the facial features of the central figure in the 1907 painting suggest that this work probably evolved from the *Wedding Day* portrait.[24] However, the later composition is a more decorative stylised work in which two women in ritualistic poses frame the central figure who holds a bowl of fruit as if engaged in some kind of quasi-sacred rite.

The earlier *Wedding Day* self portrait is a no less mysterious work. It was painted in Paris in 1906, on her fifth wedding anniversary, and she signed the painting in the bottom right hand corner with the sentence: 'I painted this aged 30 on my sixth wedding day'. Although her daughter was not conceived until spring of the following year, Modersohn-Becker appears in this painting to be visibly pregnant and is holding her stomach as if to denote the sacred nature of this part of her body. In the later work this gesture evolves into a ritualistic clasping of fruit, which often appears in her work as a symbol of growth or fertility. The 1906 portrait is a projection of her own most intimate fantasies – an attempt to convey more than just her physical self. Rilke was probably referring to this mysterious style of portraiture when, shortly after her death, he dedicated a poem to her called 'Requiem'. It includes the lines:

34   *Figure Composition, 1907*

And finally you saw yourself as fruit,
lifted yourself out of your clothes and carried
that self before the mirror, let it in
up to your gaze; which remained large, in front
and did not say: that's me, but: this is.[25]

Modersohn-Becker's paintings from the years 1905-7 become increasingly simplified and monumental in style, reflecting the influence of primitive and antique sources and French artists such as Maillol, van Gogh, Cézanne, Gauguin and the Nabis.[26] In many of the later paintings her figures appear to be set flat against the canvas surface in monumental upright or seated positions. Only occasionally does she use a traditional reclining odalisque position and her works have little in common with the more overtly erotic interpretations of the female nude by contemporary German artists such as Corinth or Böcklin. While the rounded body and tantalising pose of, for instance, Corinth's *Reclining Nude*, 1896, suggest a passive sexual availability, Modersohn-Becker emphasises the heavy dignity or primitive strength of her seated or reclining nudes.[27]

XIV
32

31

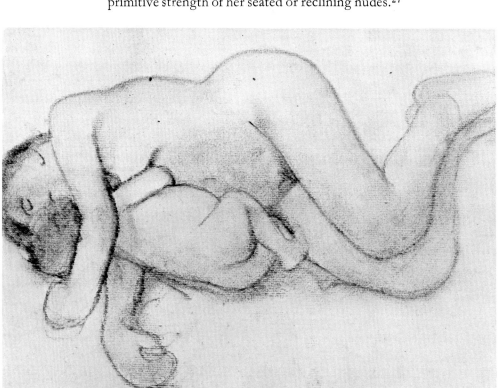

35   *Reclining Mother and Child, 1906*

Mothers with young children, mothers breastfeeding or sleeping with their young babies are some of Modersohn-Becker's favourite variations on a theme. Many of her peasant mothers are shown breastfeeding their infants, an act which she saw as a powerful and yet mysterious life-flow, and a gesture of self-sacrifice. In 1898, after drawing a Worpswede mother with her children, Paula Becker wrote in her diary:

> I've drawn a young mother with the child at her breast, sitting in her smoke filled hut . . . A sweet woman, a 'Karitas'. She was breastfeeding the large one year old bambino. And the four year old girl with the sulky eyes was snatching and grabbing at the breast until she got it. And the woman was giving her life and her youth and strength to the child in all simplicity, without realising that she was a heroic figure.

36   *Mother and Child, 1903/4*

In later paintings Paula's heroic mothers assume heavy protective dimensions and anonymous primitive features. They are often unrecognisable as individuals. This type of figure appears in the *Kneeling Mother and Child,* 1907, painted in Paris from an Italian model.

In formal terms this work would have been inconceivable without the Paris sojourn of 1906-7. The influence of Gauguin and the Nabis in the rich flat colour areas is combined with a heavy angularity reminiscent of Cézanne and, possibly, Picasso's pre-Cubist works of 1905-7. During her Paris visits Modersohn-Becker visited Ambroise Vollard's – where she first discovered Cézanne in 1900 – and other galleries along the rue Lafitte.[28] It is also possible that during later trips she visited Gertrude Stein's apartment where she could have seen contemporary works by (among others) Picasso, Cézanne and Matisse.[29] The profiled head with its heavy stylised features may have been influenced by Egyptian works in the Louvre, but the lozenge shaped eyes and the heavy lips suggest African primitive sources which also begin to appear in the work of Picasso around 1906.[30]

Through her use of warm colour harmonies Modersohn-Becker has endowed her *Kneeling Mother and Child* with what Gustav Pauli called 'a visionary quality'. He identified a luminosity which, 'like veiled moonlight envelops the scene'.[31] This atmosphere is accentuated by the strange circle of oranges which surrounds the kneeling mother. The fruit plays both a symbolic and a decorative role. Arranged like a fertility ring, it can be seen as a metaphor of growth, and the warm shades of orange counteract the purples in the woman's body.

Similar symbolic references can be found in other mother and child compositions, such as the Wuppertal and Dortmund paintings, in which both mothers and babies are holding up pieces of fruit as if to denote their greater significance. As Rilke implies in his 'Requiem', fruit was an image which could represent several associated themes:

> For that was what you understand: full fruits.
> You used to set them out in bowls before you
> and counterpoise their heaviness with colours.
> And women too appeared to you as fruit,
> and children too, both of them from within,
> impelled into the forms of their existence.[32]

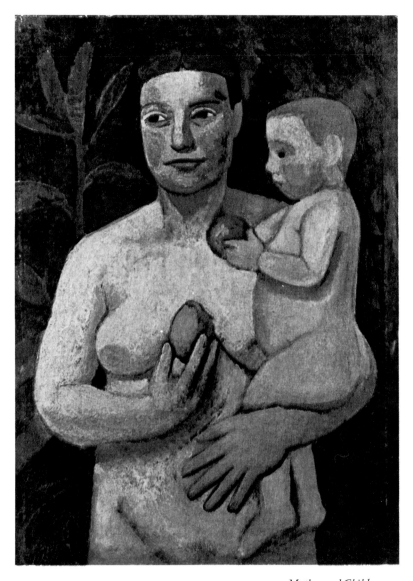

37   Mother and Child, 1907

These anonymous monumental mothers are themselves symbols of a mysterious life-giving process. In their detachment they seem to reflect something of Paula's own ambiguous attitude to motherhood.

38 Fritz Mackensen, *Mother and Infant, 1892*

While she cherished her independence in Paris and her freedom from
the domestic commitments of her home, she viewed the Worpswede
mothers with deep admiration; they are remote but heroic figures.
At the same time, motherhood is given a more personal emphasis in
the *Self Portrait on her Sixth Wedding Day* of 1906 in which she seems
to be pregnant. But even in this work the facial expression suggests
an ironic detachment from the fantasy represented by her swollen
stomach.

The mother and child theme recurs in works by other members of
the Worpswede group and it held a special interest for Fritz
Mackensen. His *Mother and Infant* of 1892, later named the 'Worpsweder Madonna', undoubtedly influenced Modersohn-Becker's

38

60

interpretations of the same theme, especially those drawings and paintings executed under Mackensen's tuition. In her painting *Peasant Woman and Child*, c1903, the sharp profile, the position of the woman's head, her tied-back hair and the suckling baby are features which echo the 'Worpsweder Madonna'. Like Mackensen,

39

Modersohn-Becker has also used a local rural setting. Her mother is set against the Worpswede moors, while Mackensen's is seated on a local peat cart.

In Mackensen's work there are quasi-religious implications. The low viewpoint, reminiscent of a Renaissance altarpiece, forces the spectator to look up at the mother and child who are, so to speak, enthroned in the cart. In the context of a north German Protestant society this work could be seen as an attempt to bring religion down to earth, to present a remote religious concept in a simple direct form. The Virgin has become an ordinary peasant, a simple 'Worpswede Madonna' who lives close to the earth.

Through the use of a higher viewpoint and a less detailed style, Modersohn-Becker, however, avoids the more sentimental connotations of Mackensen's painting, while retaining the localised references. Her peasant mother is a coarser figure painted in a bolder style which anticipates the anonymous protective figures in her *Reclining Mother and Child* of 1906 or the *Kneeling Mother and Child* of 1907.

XVIII

The Worpswede interest in this theme reflects a broader trend in German culture in the late nineteenth century. Motherhood had become a fashionable and controversial subject for debate in the 1890s. Socialist writers such as Clara Zetkin who published a pamphlet *Women Workers and the Women's Movement Today* in 1893, and Auguste Bebel whose popular *Woman, Past, Present and Future* was published in 1883, were examining the social and political role of women in modern society. They were attempting to dispel the prevalent myth that motherhood was the only calling for women. But at the same time a large amount of literature, which was appearing in the guise of anthropological or scientific study, was reinforcing the notion of woman as a kind of 'earth mother' figure whose role in life was essentially that of childbearing. Examples of this sort of pseudo-anthropological study can be found in the writings of J. J. Bachofen or H. Ploss,[33] both of whom cited historical and mythological attitudes in their attempts to evolve more modern matriarchal theories.

Although generally devoid of the sentimentality which often accompanied these views, Modersohn-Becker's powerful images of maternity clearly owe something to contemporary notions of women as 'earth mothers'. In the 1920s, when such attitudes underwent a revival in Germany, critics tended to single out the depictions of motherhood in her work, using terms like 'deep womanly quality' or 'the fervour of motherly love'[34] to describe their essential characteristics.

It is, therefore, a little ironic that later National Socialist propaganda, which attached so much importance to the virtues of motherhood and the German family, was highly critical of Modersohn-Becker's paintings. In 1935 a Nazi magazine called *Das Schwarze Korps* found her work lacking in a 'sensitive maternal quality'.[35] The crude, simplified style of many of her paintings of this theme caused the Nazis to group them with other despised examples of modern art (which included works by now hallowed artists such as Emile Nolde, Ernst Ludwig Kirchner, Max Beckmann and Oscar Kokoschka) which were purged from German museums in the late 1930s. Thus in 1937 around seventy of her works, including many mother and child compositions, were seized by the authorities and labelled 'Degenerate Art'.[36]

40   *Mother and Child, 1906*

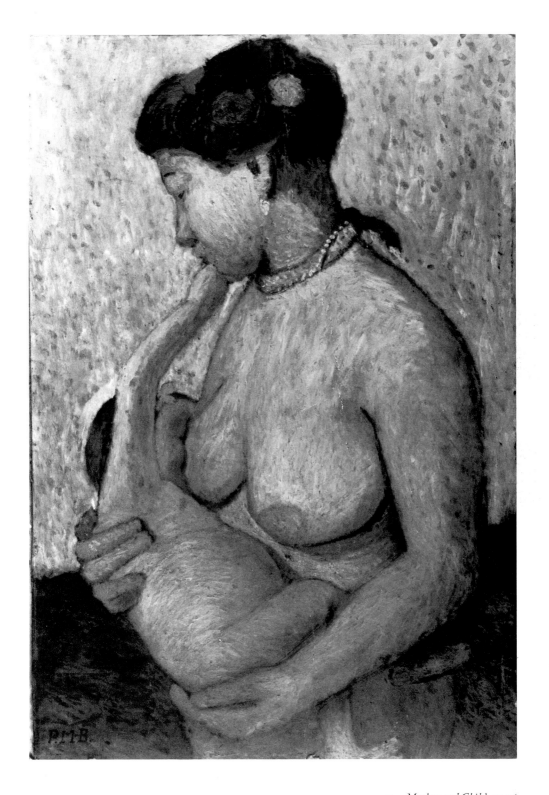

41   *Mother and Child, 1906*

1   She also visited an anatomy class at the Ecole des Beaux Arts in 1906. (See letter of 16 March 1906)

2   'Women Artists in the 20th Century: Issues, Problems, Controversies' in *Studio International,* vol. 193, no. 989, p. 165. (This article is an extract from the catalogue of the exhibition 'Women Artists: 1550-1950', Los Angeles County Museum of Art, Alfred A. Knopf, New York, 1976.

3   Kollwitz often used her graphic works as a medium for making broader points about the problems of women in German society, in particular the burdens of working class women. Such works include her 'Home Workers' series, and her many lithographs of pregnant working class women such as *At the Doctors* of 1909.

4   Letter of 10 January 1897.

5   On 2 January 1879 Bashkirtseff wrote in her diary: 'What I long for is the freedom of going out alone, of coming and going . . . that's what I long for; and that's the freedom without which one can't become a real artist . . . I must wait for my carriage, my lady companion or my family. Curse it all, it is this that makes me gnash my teeth to think I am a woman . . . This is one of the principal reasons why there are no female artists.'

6   R. Hetsch, *Ein Buch der Freundschaft,* p. 14.

7   In a letter of 10 January 1897 she describes how Haussmann encouraged her use of light and shade.

8   Letter of 30 January 1898.

9   G. Pauli, *Paula Modersohn-Becker,* Kurt Wolff, Berlin, 1934.

10 Günter Busch has discussed Modersohn-Becker and Munch in 'Uber Gegenwart und Tod – Edvard Munch und Paula Modersohn-Becker' in: *Edvard Munch, Probleme – Forschungen – Thesen,* intro. H. Boch and G. Busch, Prestel, Munich, 1973, pp. 161-76.

11 Munch was well known in Berlin artistic circles in the 1890s. He contributed 45 pictures to the Berlin Artists' Association exhibition in 1892, but the controversy aroused by his relatively advanced style caused the show to close after a few days.

12 A painted version of this work (1894-5) is in the Nasjonalgalleriet, Oslo.

13 Modersohn-Becker uses the French term 'valeurs' in a letter of 29 January 1900. Literally translated as 'values', it is used to describe the gradations of tone from light to dark.

14 She made this comment on Cola Rossi's in a letter of 19 February 1905 to Otto.

15 *Studio,* XXX, December, 1903, pp. 225-30.

16 Ibid.

17 Letter of 15 May 1900.

18 In a letter of 28 February 1905. Modersohn-Becker's courageous behaviour in Paris has also been emphasised by Ellen C. Oppler in her article 'Paula Modersohn-Becker – Some Facts and Legends' in *Art Journal*, XXXV/4, p. 365.

19 Many of Modersohn-Becker's Parisian croquis were copies of works which she saw in the Louvre during her four trips to Paris. Her 1900 Parisian sketch books include copies of several Italian early Renaissance works and between 1903 and 1906 these copies included drawings after Cranach's *Venus,* Egyptian figures, medieval tomb sculpture and Rembrandt's *Bathsheba.*

20 She discusses this drawing style in a letter of 2 March 1903.

21 Many of these watercolour drawings are now in the Musée Rodin, Paris.

22 R. M. Rilke, *Rodin* (trans. J. Lemont), Grey Walls Press, London, 1946, p. 11.

23 In her letter of 18 February 1903 she uses the metaphor of bathing her soul in cool water to convey the notion of her soul laid bare.

24 C. G. Heise has discussed the relationship between these works in *Die Sammlung des Freiherrn August von der Heydt,* Elberfeld/Leipzig, 1918. See also C. G. Heise, *Paula Becker-Modersohn: Mutter und Kind,* Philipp, Stuttgart, 1961.

25 R. M. Rilke, *Requiem and Other Poems* (trans. J. B. Leishman), London, 1949.

26 In Hetsch's *Ein Buch der Freundschaft,* Otto Modersohn has described how her studio contained reproductions of Egyptian, antique and Indian works and a large quantity of reproductions of modern French works, including paintings by Gauguin, van Gogh, Cézanne, Denis and Maillol.

27 Other works by Corinth in a similar style include his *Nacktes Mädchen im Bett,* 1893, coll. P. Leonard, Berlin, or *Die Grazien,* 1902, Bayerische Staatsgemäldesammlungen, Munich.

28 Galleries which are mentioned in Modersohn-Becker's letters include Durand Ruel (22 February 1906) and Georges Petit (15 March 1905).

29 In her book *Paula Modersohn-Becker – Kinderbildnisse,* Piper, Munich, 1977, C. Murken-Altrogge discusses the possibility that Paula may have visited Stein, p. 60, note 7.

30 There is some art historical debate as to when Picasso first used African primitive works in his paintings. However, Iberian sources probably influenced the features in his *Portrait of Gertrude Stein,* 1906, and his *Self Portrait* of the same year. Similar features can be found in his works from 1906-7 in which the 'Iberian' style leads into what Goldwater calls the 'Negro' style. See R. Goldwater, *Primitivism in Modern Art,* Vintage, New York, 1967, p.147.

31 G. Pauli, *Paula Modersohn-Becker,* p. 44.

32 R. M. Rilke, *Requiem and Other Poems.*

33 Relevant works by Bachofen have been translated into English: *Myth, Religion and Mother Right* (trans. R. Mannheim), Princeton, 1967. H. Ploss's book: *Das Weib – Natur und Völkerkunde* was published in 1897 by Griebens.

34 'Deep womanly quality' was used by O. Schürer in 'Paula Modersohn - Becker', *Der Cicerone,* 1923. Müller Wulcklow used the term 'the fervour of motherly love' in the introduction to the 1927 catalogue of the Ludwig-Roselius Sammlung in the Böttcherstrasse (Bremen).

35 *Das Schwarze Korps,* 21 August 1935.

36 In 1937 a large exhibition of works purged from German museums was held in the Archeological Institute Munich, and called 'Degenerate Art' (Entartete Kunst). The exhibition had over a million visitors in six weeks and works were surrounded with red banners covered in derisory slogans

Children

On 11 April 1905, after seeking out one of the Worpswede children whom she loved to paint, Modersohn-Becker wrote:

I looked with downright envy at all this restless new life.

Like motherhood, childhood represented an absorbing and mysterious world for Paula, a world which she often yearned to recapture. She spent hours sketching and playing with the local Worpswede children and her letters and diaries are full of comments on children who have caught her eye or inspired a painting. In 1902, after working on a painting of her step-daughter Elsbeth, she wrote to her mother, (6 July 1902):

42

It's a study of Elsbeth that I've done. She's standing in Brünjes' apple orchard, where two hens are running around, and near her stands a large flowering foxglove plant. It's not earth-shattering, of course. But with this work my creative ability and my expressive powers are growing. I definitely feel that still more good will come out of this work.

43

58

Modersohn-Becker felt that this painting represented a stylistic breakthrough. The compositional format anticipates many of her later child paintings. The figure of Elsbeth, painted in a flat, two-dimensional style, dominates the foreground picture plane. This pictorial arrangement, which is reminiscent of Max Liebermann's controversial portrait of the orphanage girl *Eva* of 1883, is developed further in later works such as the Bremen Kunsthalle *Peasant Girl Seated on a Chair,* 1905. In the Bremen painting the seated girl also occupies the front of the picture space, directly facing the spectator to form part of an almost symmetrical composition.

Modersohn-Becker's preoccupation with the child theme was nurtured on the intellectual and aesthetic interests of the Worpswede group. This theme, which had already featured prominently in paintings by Liebermann and his circle in the 1870s and 80s,[1] recurs in the work of Fritz Mackensen, Hans am Ende, Heinrich Vogeler and, to a lesser extent, Otto Modersohn.[2]

These iconographical interests are related to broader cultural ideas which were familiar within the colony. In his book *Rembrandt as Teacher*, which was avidly read by the Worpswede artists, Julius Langbehn asserted that bourgeois culture had alienated itself from the simple unsophisticated life-style that could be found in the rural peasant, and which he associated with the so-called 'Kindlichkeit' or childlike quality of uncorrupted youth. This sort of attitude encouraged the development and expansion of the German Youth Movement[3] and the idea that youth was a great regenerative force on which to build a new society. Langbehn also emphasised the power of art to revitalise society[4] and his faith in the combined potential of youth and art offered the founder members of the community (who were all in their early twenties when they first moved to Worpswede) a raison d'être for their own activities. In his monograph Rilke has described how the early members of the group felt that they were staking out 'a new life' together; as young art students they were unified in a spirit of youthful idealism.[5]

Although Modersohn-Becker was, as her sister Herma pointed out, very much 'a loner', she does at times seem to have felt a similar sense of youthful solidarity and creative freedom. While in Paris in 1900 she writes in a letter that she is spending much of her time with a group of young German artists who amuse themselves in communal activities such as singing and dancing.[6] In the same year she identifies youth with an anti-philistine freedom when she writes to her brother claiming that his mistake is to have followed too closely the ideas of an older, more traditional generation, instead of

XII

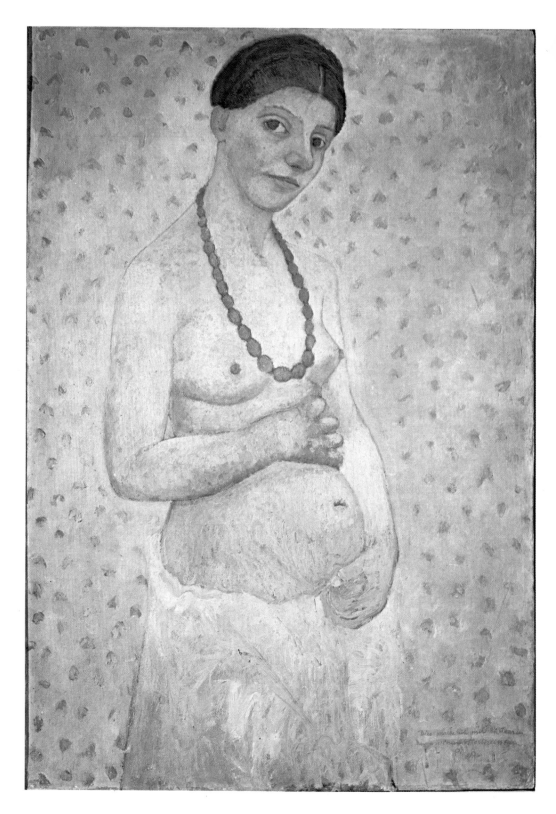

XIV

42 *Elsbeth, 1902*

following his own youthful inclinations.[7] In a similar vein, she writes in reply to a letter from her mother which had expressed concern for Paula's future, (10 November 1899):

I am still young and feel strength inside me, and I love this youth and this life too much.

A Langbehnian exaltation of youth, with its associated ideas of uninhibited creative expression, was in general opposed to the sort of sentimentality which had dominated German attitudes towards childhood in the mid-nineteenth century.[8] Similar ideas were taken up in various forms by social and educational theorists such as Ellen Key, the Swedish feminist and personal friend of Rilke. In 1902 a German translation was published of Ellen Key's book *The Century of the Child* in which she opposed an over-disciplined educational structure which, she believed, inhibited the child's creative freedom,

43 Max Liebermann, *Eva, 1883*

moulding him prematurely into a young adult. It seems highly likely that, through Rilke, Modersohn-Becker would have been aware of Ellen Key's ideas even before the two women met in Paris in 1906.[9]

Modersohn-Becker's painted and graphic interpretations of the child theme can be seen to reflect these changing attitudes. Liebermann's poorly dressed and mischievious *Eva* had marked a break with sentimentalised puppet-like figures which populated German

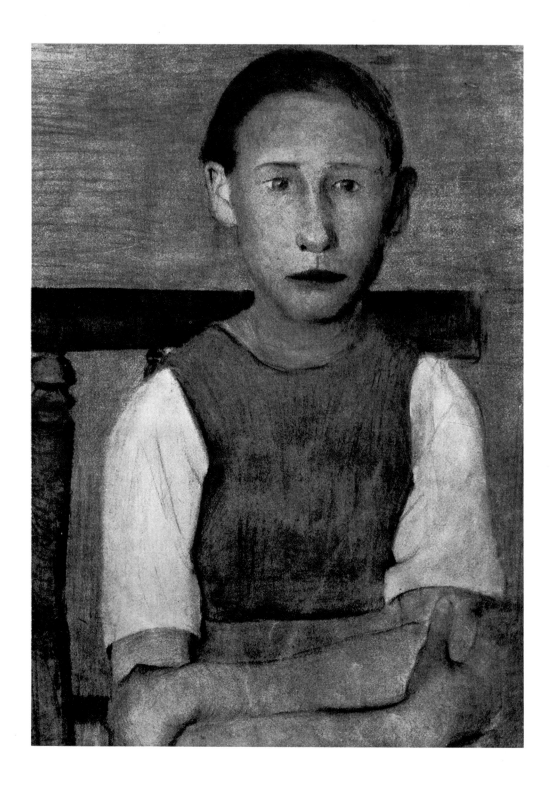

45   *Seated Girl, 1899*

genre paintings in the mid-nineteenth century. This development is
continued in Modersohn-Becker's works. Rather than show her
children in elaborate or pretty costumes, she often paints them in
simple peasant clothes, or naked with adolescent pot-bellies. Her shy,
sometimes shabby children, who seem to pursue the spectator with
their hypnotic stares, generally lack the self-conscious sweetness
which can be found in earlier interpretations of the theme by
academic German painters.[10]

This lack of sentimentality is emphasised in child studies which
show Modersohn-Becker's fascination with the more unusual or

3   *49*

40   II

46   Young Girl with Yellow Flowers in Vase, 1902

freakish characteristics of the people she saw around her in Worpswede. Just as she was attracted to the hideous dwarfish figure of Old
Dreebeen, she also found artistic potential in the chinless profile of
her *Seated Girl* of 1898/9 or in the ugliness of a young baby's face.

10   47

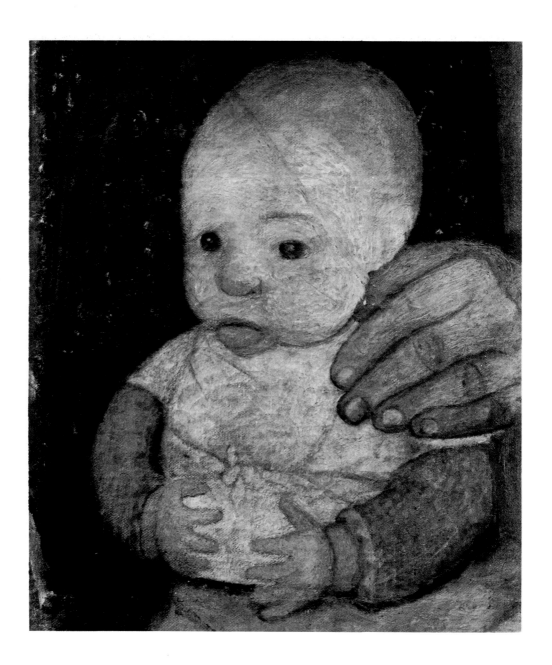

47   *Infant with Mother's Hand, 1903*

She was also preoccupied with the closely related theme of physical disability or illness.[11] In a painting of 1901, the *Portrait of a Sick Girl*, the pale young subject is placed sharply against the foreground picture plane, creating a haunting image of sickness. The theme of blindness, a disability which would have forced those afflicted with it into the village poorhouse, recurs in several of Modersohn-Becker's Worpswede subjects. Childhood blindness is illustrated in the *Blind Little Sister* of 1905 in which the older healthy girl holds her arm protectively around the younger blind child in a gesture of sisterly love.

Modersohn-Becker's fascination with physical peculiarities coexisted with a strong sense of the potential mysteries of childhood.

44

48

48 *Blind Little Sister, 1905*

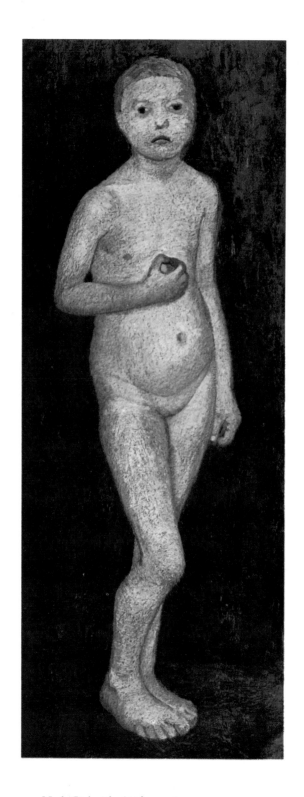

49 Nude Girl with Apple, 1906

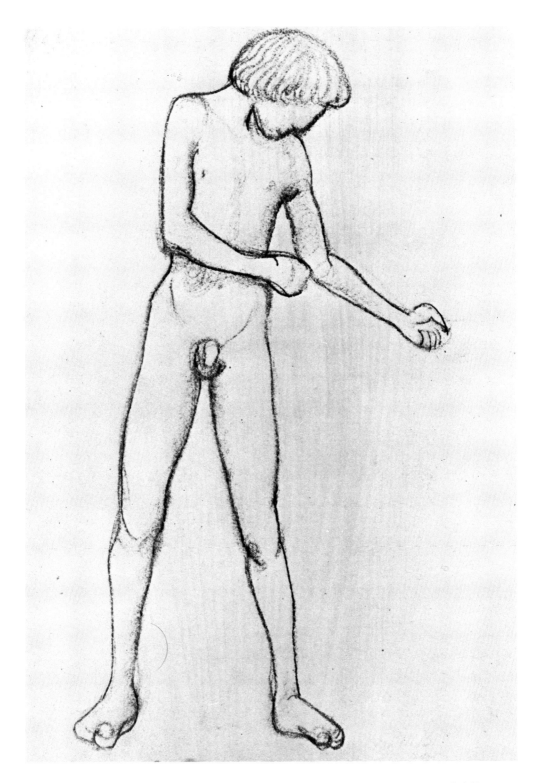

51 Ottilie Reyländer, *Sisters, 1900*

Influenced by Vogeler's wistful young girls and the romantic novels
of writers such as Gerhart Hauptmann,[12] many of her child subjects
appear to be immersed in remote dream worlds. In the 1902 painting
Elsbeth stares vacantly at the blue bells and the *Girl in front of a
Window* of 1902 and the *Girl with Pearl Necklace*,[13] also 1902, both
appear to be lost in their own distant thoughts. Her young girls can
also be found dreaming under trees in the woods, a theme which

4 55

18

echoes a form of composition popular among the circle of artists who gathered around Gauguin in Pont Aven. Paul Sérusier, Emile Bernard and Maurice Denis (whom she mentions in a letter of 28 February 1905) all used similar types of composition,[14] and it seems likely that she would have come across examples of this style of work on her regular visits to the smaller Parisian galleries around the rue Lafitte.

Child studies were an important part of the work by another young woman artist working in the colony, Ottilie Reyländer (later Reyländer-Böhme). Reyländer studied under Mackensen in 1900 and she and Paula became close friends. After a visit to Reyländer's studio in the autumn of 1900, Paula Becker wrote in her diary: 'I find the girl extremely interesting', commenting on a folder full of drawings of children and her numerous variations on the sister theme.[15]

One of Reyländer's variations on the sister theme painted in 1900, and which Modersohn-Becker must have seen in the studio, is now in the Haus im Schluh, Worpswede. This lazy pair of sisters is painted mainly in shades of earthy brown, a colour scheme encouraged by Mackensen and which is also evident in Modersohn-

52   *Two Girls in a Landscape, 1903/4*

Becker's early works painted under his tuition. The girls' long flowing hair, their wistful expressions and the gentle diagonal rhythms of the composition suggest a Jugendstil influence which is closer to Vogeler than to Modersohn-Becker. But Reyländer's repetition of the double portrait (a recurring theme in women's art[16]) probably had some influence on Paula's own iconographical preferences. She too often paints or draws two sisters, or double portraits of a girl and a boy, frequently presenting one of the figures as a shadow or silhouette of the foreground figure.

V 52

53 *Design for* Die Jugend, *1899*

54 *Design for 'La Ferme' Cigarettes, 1900*

In her sketches and graphic designs Modersohn-Becker did, on occasion, incorporate children into more stylised Jugendstil compositions. While in Berlin in March 1898 she entered (without success) a commercial design competition, writing to her family:

A series of six cards size 7 x 14 cms is required. I've supplied six girls' heads with backgrounds of stylised flowers.

The Bremen Kunsthalle design for *Die Jugend* shows the extent to which she could adapt the theme of the seated girl to create a decorative design which is devoid of the three-dimensional qualities of her contemporary drawings of Worpswede children.

53

The ornamental style of this work is developed further in her ink and watercolour design of 1900 for 'La Ferme' cigarette packets in which two young girls are playing violins in front of a row of trees. 54 While the subject matter looks forward to paintings such as the *Trumpeting Girl in the Woods* of 1903, the bold symmetrical design X anticipates those later works, such as the *Seated Nude Girl with Flowers,* 1907, in which the young girl becomes an integral part of the overall decorative composition. XXII

In her recollections of Modersohn-Becker, Ottilie Reyländer quotes her as having said in reference to painting: 'I think that I shall become more naive.'[17] This ambition was one of the features which separated the two women's work. In later child paintings from c1903 onwards, as in her work in general, Modersohn-Becker became increasingly involved in a simplified monumental style. The lozenge shaped eyes, angular features and primitive simplified bodies of many of her later nude children such as the *Girl with Stork*, 1906, the *Child with Goldfish Bowl,* 1906, or the *Nude Girl with Flowers,* 1907, clearly reflect the influences of Cézanne, Gauguin and antique and primitive works which she absorbed in Paris.

XVII
56

As in many of her self portraits and mother and child compositions, she surrounds her child subjects too with strange symbols. Apart from the obvious connotations of the stork in the *Girl with Stork*, the significance of the other decorative objects is more ambivalent. The girl is carefully positioned between two pieces of fruit, which may be included as symbols of growth. She holds a leafy twig to her chest, as if it has some magical significance, and her head is crowned with beads. She seems to represent that mysterious part of life which Paula had observed in 1905 with so deep a sense of envy.

55   Girl with Pearl Necklace, 1902

56   *Child with Goldfish Bowl, 1906*

Notes

1 The child theme also features prominently in the work of Fritz von Uhde, Hans Thoma and, to a lesser extent, Lovis Corinth. The late nineteenth century interest in this theme is often traced back to the work of the German romantic painter, Philipp Otto Runge (1777-1810), and to romantic attitudes to childhood, epitomised in Runge's much quoted statement: 'We must become children again if we wish to achieve the best.' See R. Rosenblum, *Modern Painting and the Northern Romantic Tradition,* Thames and Hudson, London, 1975, p. 50.

2 Although these artists interpreted the theme in different ways: while Mackensen and am Ende painted mainly realistic child portraits, Vogeler's dreamy children often show a strong Jugendstil stylisation.

3 In the 1890s Karl Fischer of the Steglitz Gymnasium Berlin was one of the initiators of organised hikes and outdoor activities for boys which became identified with the German Youth Movement. The organisation was based on ideas derived from educational theorists of the Pestalozzi-Montessori school, encouraging free creative expression, outdoor pursuits and proximity to nature.

4 Hence the title of Langbehn's book which identified the artist Rembrandt as a cultural symbol.

5 R. M. Rilke, *Worpswede,* Velhagen & Klasing, Bielefeld und Leipzig, 1903.

6 Letter of 4 May 1900.

7 Letter of 26 April 1900.

8 This sort of sentimentality was epitomised in Mrs Frances Hodgson Burnett's book *Little Lord Fauntleroy,* published in Germany in 1887. It was first published in England in 1886. The book was very popular in England, running into two editions in its first year of publication.

9 When they both went with Rilke on a summer trip to Chantilly. Rilke's letter describing the trip is quoted in H. W. Petzet, *Das Bildnis des Dichters,* p. 196, note to p. 82.

10 Such as Franz von Defregger or Hermann Kaulbach.

11 An interest in this theme is often identified with German Expressionism and its precursors. A disturbing recurrence of the themes of sickness or physical disabilities can be found, for example, in the work of Munch, van Gogh and Kirchner.

12 While in Worpswede, Modersohn-Becker also developed an interest in the novels of Maurice Maeterlinck. She describes this interest in a letter of 29 January 1900, writing to her father that she would like Maeterlinck's *Weisheit und Schicksal* (Wisdom and Destiny) for her birthday, describing the book as 'tranquil and soothing'.

13 This painting, in the Haus im Schluh, Worpswede, was originally part of a larger composition which included Vogeler's wife Martha holding the other end of the necklace on the child's right.

14 Similar compositions can be found in Serusier's *L'Incantation,* 1890, private collection; Bernard's *Madeleine au Bois d'Amour,* 1888, Musée d'Art Moderne Paris; Denis's *Les Muses,* 1893, Musée d'art Moderne Paris and *Paysage aux Arbres Verts,* 1893, Collection Dominique Denis. For a discussion of the French influences on Modersohn-Becker's work see C. Murken-Altrogge, 'Der Französische Einfluss im Werk von Paula Modersohn-Becker', *Die Kunst,* March, 1975, Heft 3.

15 Undated diary entry, autumn, 1900.

16 The recurrence of double portraits in women's art is discussed by Karen Petersen and J. J. Wilson in *Women Artists,* Harper and Row, New York, 1976, and The Women's Press, London, 1978.

17 R. Hetsch, *Ein Buch der Freundschaft,* p. 36.

Worpswede peat cutters later this century

Peasants

In April 1903, after returning from Paris, Modersohn-Becker commented in her diary on the 'great Biblical simplicity' of the Worpswede people. She felt both pity and admiration for their simple, stoical lives. In her first diary entry on Worpswede she had noted Fritz Mackensen's capacity to understand these people:

> He understands the peasant through and through. He knows his good qualities, he knows them all, he also knows his weaknesses. I think that he could not understand him so well had he not himself grown up in reduced circumstances.

Like the peasants, Mackensen had struggled for every penny:

> A man can never shake it off, having had to fight for pennies, not even later when he is better-off; at least the sensitive person can't. This battle leaves traces behind. They are almost invisible but there are many, many. A trained eye can detect a new one every minute. The whole person has been bound, tightly bound.

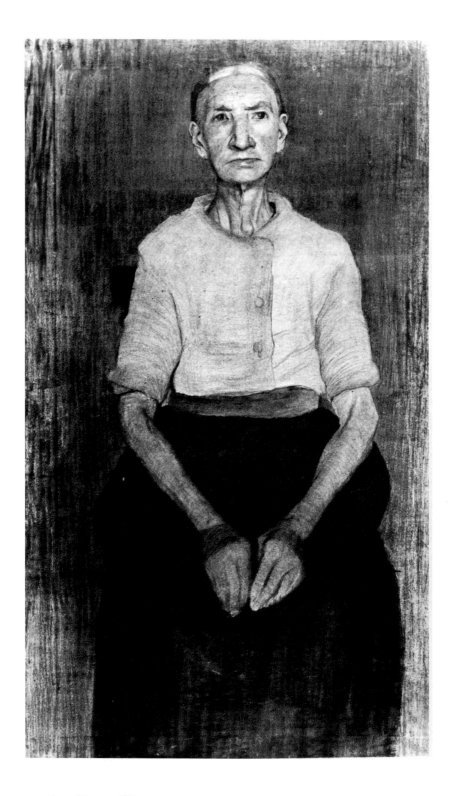

57   *Seated Peasant Woman, 1899*

58   Peasant Girl Seated on a Chair, 1905

Lack of money rivets us firmly to the ground, one's wings are
clipped.

Modersohn-Becker's attitude towards Mackensen's struggle is
ambiguous. She feels that it has curtailed his artistic drive, yet it has
also given him a resilience which she admired in the peasantry:
'He is a wonderful man . . . hard as stone and determined.'

The local peasant community played a significant part in the
Worpswede artists' decision to settle in the countryside. These
hard-working farmers and peat cutters represented unsophisticated
honest toil; they were symbols of an unchanging 'natural' life.
Such attitudes were very fashionable in Germany at the turn of the

59 *Silent Mother, 1903*

60   *Peasant Woman, 1900*

century and were championed by writers such as Paul de Lagarde[1] and Julius Langbehn. The latter's attitude to the German peasantry has been summarised by Fritz Stern:

> The peasant stood for all that remained unpolluted in society, for all that remained fixed and rooted, and his great political virtue was his cheerful subservience . . . a quality rarely encountered among 'modern' Germans.[2]

This conservative view of the peasants' stoical endurance and subservient poverty is echoed in both the written and painted works of many of the Worpswede group. Mackensen recorded local customs with minute attention to detail, endowing his peasant mother with pseudo-religious associations. Modersohn's peasants are often shown labouring peacefully in autumn landscapes; they are almost indistinguishable from the landscape around them, suggesting a 'oneness' with nature. Many of Modersohn-Becker's monumental peasant women have a heroic, timeless quality, which seems to set them above change.

Modersohn-Becker's early Worpswede drawings and paintings from 1898-1900 are sometimes categorised as belonging to her 'dark

61   Seated Peasant, 1899

62   *Peasant with Cap, 1899*

63 Peat Cutters, 1900

period', when, under Mackensen's influence, she used predominantly dark tones, perhaps to evoke the atmosphere of poverty and heavy toil appropriate to the peasant theme.

In the early peasant drawings Modersohn-Becker records individual characters who fascinated her and, occasionally, local activities such as wool spinning. While she refuses to idealise a lined or haggard face she often poses her subject as if to suggest a stoical endurance – a special dignity that comes from years of hard work. She frequently uses a sharp profile or a frontal seated portrait in which, as in the Kiel Kunsthalle drawings, the artist's eye level is below that of the sitter. Thus the spectator seems to be looking up at the subject, who acquires a monumental quality – a quality accentuated by the sitter's immobility and air of passive resignation.

12

57 61

An early painting which uses dark tones is the *Peat Cutters* of 1900 in which two peasants are cutting peat in the Worpswede moors. Echoing Mackensen's iconographical interests, she has depicted a feature of local life, but she uses more advanced formal devices to emphasise the unity of the figures and their rural setting. Both the peasants and the surrounding countryside are painted in flat areas of colour and a loose style of brushwork. Even the details of the bending man's face have been subdued as part of this overall formal pattern. The figures appear to be an integral part of the landscape.

63

The general organisation may also owe something to the French painter Millet, whose paintings of peasant subjects were very popular within the Worpswede circle.[3] In a letter of 17 January 1900, Paula wrote to Otto that Millet's works in the Louvre had particularly impressed her. Modersohn-Becker's peat cutters are isolated against a low horizon and the toiling figure of the bending worker stands out in front of a cloudy grey sky. Similar devices were used by Millet in works such as the *Angelus* (c1858-9), now in the Louvre, in which the peasants are set against an atmospheric evening sky and a low horizon.[4]

In both her drawings and her paintings Modersohn-Becker sometimes suggests the effects of exhaustive labour by drawing attention to specific physical features such as hands or eyes. Gnarled bony hands may be given a central focus within the composition, playing a symbolic or supportive role as they hold up a weary head or a walking stick.

64 67 69

In later paintings these features become increasingly simplified and in her peasant subjects from around 1902 onwards she moved further and further from the style encouraged by Mackensen, writing in her diary on 1 October 1902:

97

I believe that one should not think too much about nature when painting, at least not during the painting's conception. The colour sketch should be made exactly as one has perceived things in nature. But personal feeling is the main thing.

'Personal feeling' was an important component in Modersohn-Becker's paintings of characters from the Worpswede poorhouse. This was a local institution, similar to the British workhouse, which provided work and shelter for the poor and destitute, particularly during the winter months when work was hard to find. Regular visits to the poorhouse are well documented in her letters and diaries.[5] The place seems to have held a magical fascination for her. After one of her earliest visits with Vogeler she describes herself as arriving in 'a great Tohuwabohu',[6] and is amazed at the state of the institution and its curious inmates.

One of her favourite inmates was Old Dreebeen, the old dwarf who was also called Mutter Schröder. Paula used to chat with this strange woman, captivated by her dialect and her capacity for storytelling. After one such visit when Old Dreebeen had recounted stories in an apparently hallucinatory state, Modersohn-Becker wrote in a letter:

> Then she begins to talk about some images of her youth. But so dramatically in talk and countertalk, with varying intonation, that it is a joy to listen. One would like to put it all on paper immediately. Unfortunately I don't understand everything.[7]

Old Dreebeen's musical dialect was both a symbol of her localised peasant origins and a key to the strange world which she seemed to inhabit. Because her language was only half understood, the old woman's life was made all the more magical and impenetrable.

Old Dreebeen's mysterious appeal is well illustrated in the 1906 *Poorhouse Woman with a Glass Bowl*. Modersohn-Becker has simplified the woman's broad dimensions, reducing them to flat, decorative areas of colour, and has set her against an ornamental frieze of vertical flowers. The frieze is dominated by a large glass bowl, which echoes the rounded shape of her head. The bowl was copied from a glass bath for birds which stood in the garden in Worpswede and to which (according to Otto) Paula attached a superstitious significance.[8] Old Dreebeen is holding a foxglove as if it were a magic wand and she sits, motionless, in front of the bright red poppies. According to Gustav Pauli, she resembles an 'unworldly monster'.[9]

XV

64   *Peasant Woman with Red and Blue Headscarf, 1905*

65 *Sketch from the Tomb of Philippe Pot, 1903*

65

Pauli compares the use of distortion in this work to medieval miniatures and romanesque church sculpture, comparisons which are reinforced in Modersohn-Becker's sketches from medieval tomb sculpture and in the comments of Clara Westhoff, who has recalled her friend's interest in the carved animals in the towers of Notre Dame and the leafwork in Gothic capitals.[10]

Mutter Schröder was a favourite subject in the work of both Modersohn-Becker and Otto Modersohn. During 1902-3 they worked together regularly in the poorhouse, often spending most of their evenings there. On 13 June 1903, Otto noted in his diary:

Last night Paula really surprised me with a sketch from the poorhouse of Dreebeen, goats, chickens – marvellous as to colour, so very unusual in its conception, the surface roughened and crinkled with the paintbrush handle. Strange how large these things are, seen with great painterly vision. No one else in Worpswede interests me nearly as much as Paula. She has humour, spirit, imagination, she has a wonderful sense of colour and form. I'm full of hope.

A later painting of old Dreebeen in which Paula achieves the formal

66　*Old Woman with Handkerchief, 1906*

qualities which Otto describes is the *Poorhouse Woman by the Duck-pond* of 1904/5. Surrounded by ducks, the old woman sits and leans on her familiar stick. The rich, broad areas of colour and the rough texture of the paint surface illustrate the extent to which she had replaced Mackensen's precise style of painting with her own 'runic script'.

68

The theme of an old peasant woman watching over geese, which also recurs in Modersohn-Becker's etchings, was one which she had already admired in the work of the German painter Kalckreuth. In 1902 Modersohn-Becker commented on his painting *The Old Woman*, 1894, which she and Otto had seen in Dresden, finding in this painting something of the same 'runic' style which she sought in her own work.[11] Although Kalckreuth's painting was in many ways closer to Mackensen's peasant studies than to her own, the heavy, broad dimensions of the woman who dominates the foreground picture space, her resigned expression and her haggard features clearly appealed to Modersohn-Becker and may have influenced her own compositions.

13

In earlier variations on this theme, such as her etching, *The Goosegirl*, 1899/1900, she was greatly influenced by Vogeler's Jugendstil prints. In 1895 Vogeler, am Ende, Mackensen and Overbeck had purchased a printing press which they installed in the Barkenhoff. Under Vogeler's guidance Paula Becker used the press in her own series of etchings from 1899–1900.

Another of her favourite poorhouse subjects was a curious character called von Bredow, the destitute son of a Prussian nobleman. On 4 October 1898 she wrote:

> Old Bredow from the poorhouse, he has had such a life! Now he lives in the poorhouse and looks after the cow. Years ago his brother wanted to make him part of proper society. But the old man had grown so fond of his cow and his dreaming. He won't let go of that. Now he holds the cow on a lead, walks with her on the yellow-grey meadow, gives her a tap with his stick at every step, and philosophises. He studied. Then he was a grave digger during the cholera in Hamburg. Then for six years he was a sailor, and on the whole probably had a wild life, fell to drinking to forget and now has found evening-peace in the poorhouse.

Von Bredow would seize every opportunity to recount his life story to Paula. He seemed all the more pitiful for having been well educated and of a noble family. In her drawing of 1898-9 she shows

67   *Old Bredow, 1899*

him in profile, holding his stick, now with almost no trace of his original aristrocratic expression. Modersohn-Becker's lengthy description suggests that she was irresistibly drawn towards this strange character. Like Old Dreebeen, he was a source of physical idiosyncrasies and endless stories which were alien to her own more fortunate life.

After visiting the poorhouse in 1898, Paula wrote in a letter to her family: 'I find it so strange in these surroundings' (18 September). Old Dreebeen, Old Bredow and the other peculiar inmates who attracted her attention,[12] provided artistic inspiration precisely because they were so odd and so remote. For Paula, their lined faces and ugly bodies represented a stoical endurance rather than a social malaise; they are the silent occupants of a barely penetrable world.

68   Leopold von Kalckreuth, *The Old Woman, 1894*

69 *Old Peasant, 1903*

1   Paul de Lagarde (1827-91) was a theologian and scholar who, like Langbehn, criticised modern German society seeking salvation in a spiritual regeneration and in an indigenous German 'Volk'. In 1878 he published his *Deutsche Schriften,* a collection of essays on general subjects which included theology and German culture.

2   F. Stern, *The Politics of Cultural Despair,* Anchor, New York, 1965, p. 189.

3   Modersohn, Mackensen and Vogeler were all admirers of Millet's work, which became reasonably well-known in Germany in the late nineteenth century. Rilke also cites this influence on the Worpswede works in his *Worpswede* monograph, p. 10.

4   Modersohn-Becker does not, however, romanticise her subject in the manner of Millet's heroic peasant studies. She avoids the atmospheric effects evoked by the red evening sky.

5   See her letters of 18 September 1898; 4 October 1898; 15 December 1898; 27 June 1902.

6   Letter of 18 September 1898.

7   Ibid.

8   R. Hetsch, *Ein Buch der Freundschaft,* p. 20.

9   G. Pauli, *Paula Modersohn-Becker,* pp. 42-3. This painting has often been compared to van Gogh's *La Berceuse,* 1889, Sammlung Rudolf Staechelin, Kunstmuseum Basel. The bright colouring in Modersohn-Becker's picture may also reflect the influence of Fauve works which she had seen in Paris. In a letter of 24 March 1905 she comments on the Salon des Indépendants which included 'dull convention next to extreme Pointillisme'. Fauve works were well represented in the 1906 Salon d'Automne, which also included the Gauguin retrospective.

10 R. Hetsch, *Ein Buch der Freundschaft,* p. 43.
    Modersohn-Becker also mentions her interest in the Gothic stone-work on Notre Dame in a letter from Paris written on 29 February 1900.

11 Diary entry of 1 December 1902.

12 These included characters such as 'die alte Olheit', an old woman from Bremen (see letter of 15 December 1898), and 'Mutter Meyer', a woman who had been maltreated by her husband (see same letter).

Landscape and Still Life

Landscape paintings were among the first of Paula Becker's works to be exhibited in public. She contributed mostly dark-toned moor scenes to the 1899 Worpswede exhibition in Bremen Kunsthalle[1] and does not seem to have been unduly perturbed by Fitger's dismissive criticism, recording tersely in her diary:

> In December 1899, the first exhibition of my pictures in the Kunsthalle Bremen.[2]

Between 1899 and c1903 she painted many Worpswede landscapes which, under the influence of works by Otto Modersohn and Fritz Overbeck, use high horizons, steeply receding ditches or canals and strong blues and greens in the colouring. Other motifs which recur in these early landscapes include the steep pitched roofs of Worpswede barns and cottages, slender birch trees (her 'young women') and sturdy pine trees (her 'mighty men').

Modersohn-Becker adopted the motifs rather than the sentimental mood which characterised the landscape style of many of the

70 *Glade, 1900*

71   Barn against an Evening Sky, 1900

Worpswede painters. She avoided the poetic mood evoked by
Modersohn's atmospheric moor scenes, concentrating instead on the
formal possibilities of her subject. She used flat, roughly painted
colour areas and shortened perspective, and the tree trunks are often
used to create two-dimensional designs rather than suggest three-
dimensional recession.

8   70

Not surprisingly, Mackensen was critical of this landscape style.
Not only was Paula moving away from the common Worpswede
aim of the 'secret of a mood' (Stimmungsgeheimnis) in painting,[3] but
she was also sacrificing the painstaking observation of nature which
was the backbone of Mackensen's teaching. Even Modersohn,
despite his own experiments with a freer landscape style, criticised
her landscapes after the Bremen exhibition, finding them lacking in
intimacy and 'too poster-like'.[4]

Despite these differences, Modersohn-Becker shared many of the
attitudes which the Worpswede group held towards nature. The
colony had been formed as an attempt to get back to a simple
unsophisticated life in a 'natural' environment. For the founder

72 Boy with Grazing Goat, 1902

members of the group, nature was a concept which sometimes assumed a quasi-religious significance. This is emphasised by Rilke in his monograph, when he compares the Worpswede attitudes with those of the early nineteenth century German romantic painters, in particular Philipp Otto Runge, for whom nature represented a mystical, even religious force.[5] According to Rilke, the Worpswede artists went out into the countryside feeling that every leaf contained within itself a part of 'the great laws of the universe'.[6]

A sense of the potential power of nature is echoed in several of Modersohn-Becker's written comments. In 1898 she remarked of Mackensen: 'He is often hard and egotistical. But before nature he is a child.'[7] Mackensen feels humble before the omnipotence of nature. Other remarks suggest that she herself often felt possessed by some kind of natural force. While in Norway in the summer of 1898 she recorded her reactions to the local scenery, describing the sensations which she felt while lying alone under a tree:

73   *View from the Artist's Studio Window in Paris, 1900*

I was lying under the alder tree. My soul was completely under its spell. I looked up into its leaves. The sun dyed them a shining yellow. And thus they stood on their delicate red stems and laughed into the sky.

In December that year in Worpswede she reacted in a similar way to moonlight on the snow, feeling a personal communion with nature:

This indescribably sweet web of moonlight and delicate snowy ether that surrounded me. Nature was talking to me and I listened, trembling with bliss.

Modersohn-Becker's love of the countryside caused her to react unfavourably to the crowded urban environment of Paris when she first arrived there in 1900. She comments in her diary on the dirty depressing atmosphere and in her first letter home she writes of a dreadful feeling which 'wells up' inside her in these surroundings.[8]

Despite her initial yearnings for the rural environment she had left behind, she soon adjusted to her new surroundings, immersing herself in her art and, instead of landscapes, occasionally painting and (particularly during later visits) sketching cityscapes. Thus in 1900 she adapts her landscape style to interpret a different scene in her *View from the Artist's Studio Window in Paris*, probably the view from her hotel room in the Grand Hôtel de la Haute Loire on the boulevard Raspail.[9] The painting has a dark-toned 'poster-like' quality which can also be found in her Worpswede landscapes from the same period.[10]

Modersohn-Becker often used landscapes as settings for figure groups, as in *The Good Samaritan,* 1907, a rare example of a religious theme in her work. This painting, which is strikingly similar to some of Wassily Kandinsky's Murnau landscapes,[11] is indebted to French sources which she absorbed during her final year in Paris. The flat areas of rich colour outlined in black are reminiscent of Gauguin's syntheticist works, many of which were exhibited in his 1906 Memorial Exhibition.

73

XXIV

Still Life

In the years after c1903, Modersohn-Becker painted few simple landscapes (although she continued to paint the theme of figures in landscapes), concentrating increasingly on her still lifes. These play a central role in her artistic development towards 'great simplicity of form'. In her paintings the colours, shapes and surfaces of objects assumed a significance beyond their purely representational references. According to Heinrich Vogeler: 'The colour, the form of the object communicated something to her'; she would 'immerse' herself in the object.[12]

Each part of a still life composition was subject to its own formal laws, laws which she felt she could somehow penetrate through painting. In a letter of 25 February 1903 she wrote to Otto that through drawing she must seek out nature's remarkable forms, commenting:

I have a feeling for the interlacing and the layering of objects. I must develop and refine this carefully.

This refining process is the product of close observation. On 20 February 1903, after explaining the 'gentle vibration of things'

75   *Still Life with Blue and White Porcelain, 1900*

Still Life with Chestnuts, 1905

which she sought in her paintings, she asserts with conviction the
broad aim of her work:

> Generally through the most intimate observation to aspire to the
> greatest simplicity.

Her attempts to penetrate the inner quality of an object were
closely bound up with a formal process of simplification and
reconstruction. The development of this process can be traced in a
comparison of her earliest still lifes, such as the 1900 *Still Life with
Blue and White Porcelain*, with works from after 1903, such as the *Still
Life with Chestnuts*, 1905, or the *Still Life with Pumpkin*, 1905. While
the earlier painting is characterised by a delicate drawing style,
lighter tones and a loose, more impressionistic application of paint,
the later still lifes generally use stronger colours and clearer, more
compact groups of objects. In this way Modersohn-Becker has
'refined' and reconstructed her objects, reducing them to simplified

75

76 78

77   Still Life with Sunflower, 1907

arrangements of forms and colours. In her latest interpretations of
this theme from 1906-7 she often uses a flat, two-dimensional style
with clear outlines and bright colours which echoes the style of Emile
Bernard's still lifes from the late 1880s.[13] The influence of van Gogh
is also clearly in evidence in her *Still Life with Sunflower* of 1907 in
which the subject matter, the brushwork and the colouring are very
close to van Gogh's *Sunflowers* of 1888, now in the National Gallery,
London.

81

77

Modersohn-Becker's attempt somehow to penetrate the inner qualities of different objects may have been influenced by the theoretical concepts which interested her immediate circle of friends, in particular Modersohn and Rilke. In a diary entry of 1 July 1901 Modersohn discusses the need for simplification in the expression of 'the object in itself in feeling' (Das Ding an sich in Stimmung).[14] Although neither Otto nor Paula developed these ideas on a deeper philosophical level, they seem to have shared a sense of the need to represent the most 'intimate' qualities of each inanimate object.

Rilke, through his growing interest in the visual arts and his association with Rodin, was evolving similar (though more complex) theories of representation. Under the influence of Rodin he evolved a notion of the object (das Ding) and its intrinsic meaning as the product of careful craftsmanship,[15] extending this theory to apply it to his style of writing.[16]

79   Still Life with Fruit, 1905

Both Modersohn-Becker and Rilke shared an influence, the work of Paul Cézanne, which was instrumental in bringing about modifications and developments in their respective attitudes to art. Around 1907 Rilke became very involved in Cézanne's paintings, in which he found an art which conveyed the inner character of a subject.[17] Modersohn-Becker was first impressed by Cézanne's works when she visited Vollard's gallery in Paris in 1900. This discovery has been described by Clara Westhoff:

> One day Paula invited me to join her on a walk to the other bank of the Seine to show me something special there. She led me to the art dealer Vollard... Paula had discovered him [Cézanne] in her own way, and this discovery was for her an unexpected confirmation of her own artistic searchings.[18]

118

In a letter of 21 October 1907 to Clara, Modersohn-Becker recalls the impression which this visit made on her, describing Cézanne as 'one of the three or four French painters who has acted upon me like a thunderstorm'. In a letter which she wrote the following day to her mother, she expresses a deep desire to see 'the 56 Cézannes' exhibited in a retrospective show in Paris that year.

In Cézanne's still lifes she found a new expression of form which had abandoned an impressionist emphasis on atmosphere and transitory impressions, in favour of a clear sense of structure and composition. The influence of the French painter is in evidence in paintings such as the Bremen Kunsthalle *Still Life with Fruit,* 1905, or the *Still Life with Apples and Green Glass,* 1906, in the Ludwig-Roselius Collection, Bremen. In these works there are links with Cézanne in the compositional structure, the use of coloured planes and the lack of tactile distinctions between different surfaces and objects. The folds in the tablecloth, the uneasy perspective and tilted viewpoints of the Bremen *Still Life with Fruit* are features which can

79
80

80   *Still Life with Apples and Green Glass, 1906*

also be found in Cézanne's *Still Life with Apples and Oranges* of c1895, now in the Jeu de Paume Museum, Paris.

The *Still Life with Apples and Green Glass* was one of the very few paintings which Modersohn-Becker sold during her lifetime. It was bought in 1906 by Vogeler who wrote in his autobiography that he hung the painting in the Barkenhoff 'and sent a small sum of money to Paula in Paris'.[19] The 'small sum of money' must have been particularly welcome in 1906. Being financially dependent on Otto, she found it difficult to make ends meet and was forced to borrow money from Rilke.[20]

Modersohn-Becker's still lifes share a strange static quality. Her bowls, plates, jugs, fruit and flowers all seem to possess an immobile, lifeless character that is perhaps best conveyed by the French term 'nature morte'. Rather than create a sense of life and atmosphere in these works, she tended to concentrate increasingly on the construction of the design and the formal characteristics of each component part. Each inanimate object acquires its own special quality within the design; a pumpkin, a boiled egg, a glass or a sunflower exists as a separate entity with its own special characteristics of form and colour, before it forms part of a still life group.

81   Still Life with Pottery Jug, 1906

Notes

1   The Bremen Kunsthalle handwritten inventory from December 1899
    mentions only two of Paula Becker's exhibits by name: *Evening* and
    Pond. Her other exhibits are grouped under the title 'collection'.
2   This entry appears only in the 1920 edition of the *Briefe und Tage-
    buchblätter,* under a probably erroneous date of 17 December 1901.
3   Quoted in Otto Stelzer, *Paula Modersohn-Becker*, Rembrandt, Berlin,
    1958, p. 12.
4   Diary entry of 27 January 1901. This is quoted in the appendix to the
    1920 edition of the *Briefe und Tagebuchblätter,* p. 248.

5 In a much quoted letter of 9 March 1802, Runge wrote: 'When the heavens above me teem with countless stars, the wind soars through the expanse of space, the wave breaks with a foaming roar in the vast night, the ethereal sky reddens above the wood and the sun lights up the world, the valley is filled with mist and I throw myself down on grass amid sparkling dew-drops, every leaf and every blade of grass teems with life, the earth is alive and moves under me, everything is sounding the same chord simultaneously, then the soul shouts for joy, and flies in the immeasurable space around me, there is no below and no above any more, no time, no beginning and no end. I hear and feel the living breath of God who holds and bears the world, in whom everything lives and works.' Quoted in U. Finke, *German Painting from Romanticism to Expressionism*, p.17.

6 Rilke, *Worpswede*, p.13.

7 Diary entry of 29 October 1898.

8 Letter of 1 January 1900.

9 This is the room which she mentions in the same letter (note 8).

10 Günter Busch has compared this work with background of Josef Rippl-Ronai's *Portrait of Aristide Maillol* now in the Jeu de Paume Museum, Paris. See *Paula Modersohn-Becker zum Hundertsten Geburtstag*, Bremen, 1976, cat. no. 18.

11 Painted while he and Gabriele Münter were living in the village of Murnau near Munich in 1908–10. It is very unlikely that Kandinsky would have been aware of works by Modersohn-Becker. The stylistic parallels are more likely the product of both artists having absorbed similar French influences.

12 'Paula Modersohn-Becker', *Literarischen Monatschrift*, 11, Drittes Jahr, 1938.

13 Notable examples include his *Still Life with Blue Coffee Jug*, 1888 Bremen Kunsthalle, and his *Still Life with Cherries*, 1887, private coll. (Altarriba) Paris.

14 Cited in *Otto Modersohn 1865–1943*, Otto Modersohn-Museum Fischerhude, 1977, opposite plate 224.

15 Rilke's continually evolving notion of 'das Ding' is discussed at length in K. Batterby, *Rilke and France*, Oxford University Press, London, 1966.

16 See Rilke's letter to Lou Andreas Salomé of 10 August 1903, in which he relates these theories to his writing. This letter is cited in the introduction to Rilke's *Briefe über Cézanne*, Insel, Frankfurt, 1952.

17 These ideas are discussed in K. Batterby, *Rilke and France*, pp. 82, 88.

18 R. Hetsch, *Ein Buch der Freundschaft*, p.43.

19 H. Vogeler, *Erinnerungen*, p. 143.

20 In a letter of 30 June 1906 to Otto, she expresses delight at the fact that Otto has sold another one of her still lifes, but says that unfortunately she must use the money to repay 100 marks to Rilke.

Portraits and Self Portraits

On 23 April 1896, in her first year at the Berlin School of Art for Women, Paula Becker described her enthusiasm for portrait studies:

> I study physiognomies on my way to classes with great pleasure, trying to find quickly what's characteristic in them. When I'm talking to someone I observe diligently what kind of shadow the nose is throwing and how the deep shadow on the cheek stands out strongly and then melts into the light.

The portrait was a medium through which she could both capture and interpret the essential characteristics of her subjects who included the anonymous models she sketched and painted while studying in Berlin and Paris, local Worpswede peasants and close friends.

In the period 1905-6 Modersohn-Becker worked on several portraits of her closest friends, including her sister Herma, Clara Westhoff, Rilke, the sociologist Werner Sombart and Lee Hoetger, the wife of the sculptor Bernhard Hoetger. In Worpswede in the autumn of 1905 she painted Clara Westhoff, noting in her diary on

82   Sketch for Portrait of Clara Rilke-Westhoff, 1905

83   *Clara Rilke-Westhoff, 1905*

26 November that Clara was wearing a white dress and holding a red rose. Paula goes on to comment: 'She looks very beautiful . . . Despite everything, she is still the one I love most.' In this last sentence she is reaffirming the strength of her feelings for Clara, after a break which had occurred in 1901. While they were working together in Worpswede between 1898 and 1900 the two women built up a very close friendship, spending much of their leisure time together and sharing similar views on art and nature. However, Paula reacted dramatically when, after her marriage to Rilke in the spring of 1901 (shortly before Paula's own wedding), Clara moved away from Worpswede and seemed to immerse herself in her new life with her husband. Paula felt that Rilke was keeping his wife in chains, and her feelings of jealousy and unhappiness are revealed in a poignant letter which she wrote to her friend in the autumn of 1901, using Clara's maiden name and the formal pronoun 'Sie':

> . . . And I whose attitude to life is different, I was hungry. Is love then not manifold? Must it give everything to the one? And take from others?
>
> Should love take? Is it not much too gracious, too great, too all-embracing? Clara Westhoff, why don't you live as nature lives. The deer group together in herds, the little tits outside our window have their community, and not just the family.
>
> I read you with a little sadness. From your words Rilke speaks too strongly and too passionately. Does love then demand that one should become like the other? No, a thousand times no! Is not the union of two strong persons so rich and full of happiness because both serve in humility and peace and joy and quiet contentment?
>
> I know little about you two, but it seems to me that you have shed much of your old self in order to lay it at the feet of your king like a cloak for him to walk over. For yourself, for the world, for art, and for me as well, I would like you to wear your gilded mantle again.

By the time Modersohn-Becker came to paint Clara's portrait in 1905, this early rift, though not forgotten, was a thing of the past. The portrait represents a personal impression of Clara. In the 1905 diary entry Paula talks of her friend's beauty, a beauty which is symbolised by the red rose. Clara's strong features are emphasised by the clear white dress and the dark background. Her eyes are focussed to the side and her head is tilted slightly back, suggesting an aloofness or emotional distance.

By 1905 Clara's relationship with Rilke had lost some of its earlier intensity. Rilke and Paula grew closer during her visits to Paris in 1903 and 1905. The somewhat ambivalent relationship which developed between Paula, Clara and Rainer Maria has been much discussed by Rilke's biographers and, perhaps, oversimplified in glib statements such as 'Rilke's double romance with Clara and Paula'.[1] Although there are large gaps in Modersohn-Becker's surviving correspondence from the years 1903-7, Rilke's letters indicate that he and Paula spent much time together in Paris in 1906,[2] the year in which she painted his portrait.[3] Rilke left Paris in   XVI
July 1906 not knowing, of course, that he would never see Paula again.

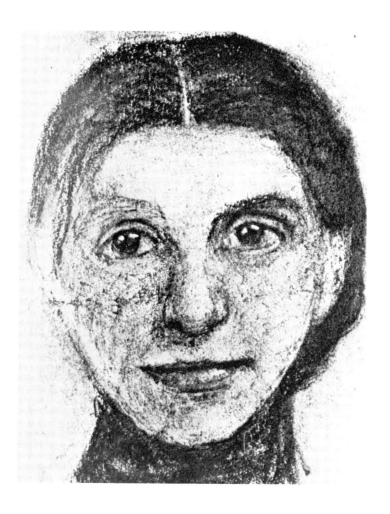

84 Self Portrait, 1903

85   *Woman with a Poppy, 1900*

86 *Herma, 1906*

87 Clara Rilke-Westhoff, *Rainer Maria Rilke, 1936*

The painting of Rilke, with its emphasis on the two-dimensional canvas surface and simplified features, marks an important development in Modersohn-Becker's portrait style which echoes a diary entry of 25 February 1903:

> All along I have been striving to give the heads which I drew or painted the simplicity of nature. Now I feel deeply how I can learn from antique heads. How they are seen in the large and with such simplicity! Forehead, eyes, mouth, nose, cheeks, chin, that is all.

87

A comparison of this portrait with Clara Westhoff's bronze head of Rilke illustrates the extent to which Modersohn-Becker had simplified and reconstructed her subject's face, concentrating on the eyes, the nose and the open mouth. This painting, as with the portrait of Clara, is her personal statement about Rilke.

88 *Werner Sombart, 1906*

The style of the Rilke portrait is similar to that of several other portraits painted in the same year: *Werner Sombart, Herma,* her sister, and *Lee Hoetger.* Werner Sombart was a well-known sociologist whom Modersohn-Becker met during a visit to Carl Hauptmann's house in January 1906. In a letter to her sister Milly she writes of the pleasant and interesting circle of people gathered there, describing the learned discussions between Hauptmann and Sombart.[4] In the portrait Sombart's clear staring eyes and heavy beard suggest the

88 86

XIX XX

89 Young Woman with Red Hat, 1900

90   *Self Portrait with White Necklace, 1906*

intense intellectual qualities which so impressed Modersohn-Becker, while the flat areas of colour and the simplified features anticipate the painting of Rilke. Although more prominent in the Sombart picture, both these works share a use of strange red outlines, a device which may have been influenced by some of van Gogh's portraits.[5]

These red outlines also appear in the portait of *Herma,* probably painted during a trip to Britanny at Easter 1906. Herma was nearly ten years younger than Paula, a fact which is reflected in a letter of 9 March 1906 to Otto, in which Paula writes that she sees her sister (who was studying languages in Paris) only occasionally, and that Herma 'has much to learn'. The young Herma is painted with a youthful rounded face, holding a flower in her left hand, which breaks the symmetry of an otherwise simple composition.

An even stronger symmetry dominates the portrait, *Lee Hoetger,* now in the Ludwig-Roselius Collection, Bremen. This is one of three portraits of Hoetger's wife painted by Paula in Paris in 1906.[6] In this brightly coloured painting she sets the monumental figure of Lee Hoetger between two groups of flowers in a manner strongly reminiscent of the 'primitive' compositions of Henri (le Douanier) Rousseau, who was a personal friend of the Hoetgers. On 31 July 1906, Modersohn-Becker wrote in her diary that she had just finished the portrait of Frau Hoetger:

> The woman interests me and she becomes more and more dear to me. She has something grandiose about her and she's quite splendid to paint.

While in Paris in 1906–7 Modersohn-Becker often visited the Hoetgers. From Bernard Hoetger she received understanding and inspiration. As a sculptor, he encouraged her to pursue the monumental style which characterises, for example, the portrait of his wife in the garden and many of the later self portraits.

'Why should one paint oneself over and again? There is a quite simple explanation: this model is always available', writes Tatiana Ahlers-Hestermann in her discussion of Modersohn-Becker's self portraits.[7] Models generally cost money, particularly in the competitive Parisian art world, and Modersohn-Becker's financial resources were limited. But she also seems to have used the self portrait as a vehicle for continual self-exploration.[8] Although they rarely suggest any deep psychological analysis, these works present the artist in a

XVII

XVIII

XX

XXI

XXII

XXIII   XXIV

XXV

91   *Self Portrait with Hand on Chin, 1906*

variety of attitudes, poses and moods. The introspective haunting expressions of some of her earliest self portraits are superceded by the confident nude self portraits of 1906-7 in which she herself often assumes the monumental proportions of her heroic peasant mothers.

In 1932 Ottilie Reyländer recalled the pronounced nature of Paula's facial features, which gave to her 'little head' a strong forceful quality.[9] Even in Modersohn-Becker's earliest self portraits, in which the semi-impressionistic style blurs the contours, these strong features are apparent. In a self portrait painted in Paris in 1900 the face is painted from a strange viewpoint, creating a curious sense of distortion. She is looking up at herself from below and her eyes suggest distant or introspective thoughts, an expression which can also be found in several of Gwen John's self portraits.[10]

Modersohn-Becker continually used self portraits as vehicles for her formal experiments. With the model ever present, she was able to dwell at length on formal problems and new techniques, as in her *Self Portrait* of 1903 in which she pulled the paintbrush handle along the paint surface, creating the rough 'coarse grained' texture which she described in her letter of 20 February of the same year.[11] This portrait, like many of those of young children, is presented as a simple frontal view and the spectator is drawn into the painting by Modersohn-Becker's hypnotic stare. But the artist still remains distant; there is a note of mystery in her staring eyes.

A sense of mystery also pervades her famous *Self Portrait with Camellia Branch* of 1907 in which the strong compositional symmetry and the dark, mask-like face was probably influenced by Egyptian mummy portraits.[12] The lower centre of the composition is dominated by her unfinished hand and the camellia branch which she holds up in front of her in a strange ritualistic gesture.

Several of her written comments suggest that flowers had a special role to play in the self portraits. Although the precise nature of their symbolism is ambiguous, different flowers seem to have had specific personal associations for Modersohn-Becker. In a diary entry of 24 February 1902 she envisages her future grave decorated with white carnations, having had an earlier premonition of premature death. Death, flowers and her love of painting were closely associated in her moving diary entry of 26 July 1900:

I know I shall not live very long. But why is that so sad? Is a festival more beautiful because it lasts longer? My sensuous perceptions grow sharper, as if I were supposed to take in everything within the few years that will be offered to me ... And now

136

92　*Self Portrait with Camellia Branch, 1907*

love will still blossom for me before I depart, and if I've painted three good pictures, then I shall leave gladly with flowers in my hand and my hair.

XXI

In 1906 she painted herself twice with flowers in her hand and her hair. These two similar self portraits are now in the Ludwig-Roselius Collection and the Kunstmuseum Basel. In both these half-length portraits she is naked, crowned with pink flowers and wearing an amber necklace; the warm pinks and oranges are set against the rich blues and greens of the background frieze. She has become a remote monumental figure.

91

93

Hands share with flowers an important symbolic and formal role in Modersohn-Becker's self portraits. Unlike the withered, supportive hands of her peasants, they often assume a probing or reflective gesture in her self portraits. In the Hannover and Ludwig-Roselius Collection self portraits they are resting lightly on the chin, as if to suggest personal reflection. Her sketchbooks contain many individual studies of hands for, like the human face, she believed that they could tell much about a person's life and character.

During the last few months of her life, Modersohn-Becker's pregnancy made it increasingly difficult for her to work. She gave birth to her daughter Mathilde on 2 November 1907. On 21 November, as she got up from her bed for the first time, she suffered a thrombosis of the leg and a fatal heart attack.

She died at the point at which she was beginning both to fulfill her own artistic ambitions and to receive some favourable criticism. When she exhibited for the second time at the Worpswede show in Bremen Kunsthalle in the winter of 1906, her work was praised by Gustav Pauli, the museum director and organiser of the show. In his review of 11 November 1906, published in the newspaper *Sonntag,* he admired her sophisticated use of colour and powerful decorative style, describing her as 'a highly gifted woman artist'. Modersohn-Becker was in Paris when she heard about the review. On 18 November 1906 she wrote to her sister:

The criticism gave me satisfaction rather than pleasure. The real pleasures, the overwhelmingly beautiful hours, are experienced through art, without being noticed by others. The same applies to the sad ones. That's why in art one is usually totally alone with oneself. But the review is good for my Bremen début and may perhaps shed a different light on my departure from Worpswede.

The initial lack of understanding which she encountered from family and friends, and her divergences from the artistic aims of the Worpswede circle, had caused her to work for herself, finding her 'real pleasures' when she was alone with her painting. By 1907 she had achieved her 'great simplicity of form' in works such as the *Kneeling Mother and Child* or the *Self Portrait with Amber Necklace*. XXV
She had realised her feeling, expressed to her mother in a letter of XXI
6 July 1902, that:

> Soon the time will come when I won't need to be ashamed and keep quiet but I shall feel with pride that I am a painter.

1 From an English biography (unnamed) cited by H. W. Petzet in *Das Bildnis des Dichters,* p.20.

2 See R. M. Rilke, *Briefe aus den Jahren 1902–6.* Much of this correspond-ance is also cited in Petzet, *Das Bildnis des Dichters,* pp. 88ff.

3 There is some disagreement over the dating of this portrait. Petzet (p.138) claims that it was painted between 13 May and 2 June 1906, although it has also been dated as 1905.

4 Letter of 17 January 1906.

5 As in, for example, van Gogh's portrait, *Camille Roulin,* 1888.

6 The second of these portraits, now in the Graphisches Kabinett Bremen, has been compared in style with Picasso's *Portrait of Gertrude Stein* of 1906. See C. Murken-Altrogge 'Der Französische Einfluss im Werk von Paula Modersohn-Becker'.

7 *Paula Becker-Modersohn: Mutter und Kind* (intro. C. G. Heise), p. 14.

8 In this respect they might be compared with the self portraiture of contemporary artists such as Lovis Corinth and Vincent van Gogh. However, Modersohn-Becker's self portraits have little in common with the psychological intensity to be found in van Gogh's paintings.

9 R. Hetsch, *Ein Buch der Freundschaft,* p. 32.

10 This sense of aloofness, partly created through a low viewpoint, is paralleled in Gwen John's *Painting by Herself* (Self Portrait), 1900, now in the National Gallery, London.

11 See 'Images of Women'.

12 G. Busch has identified the influence of Coptic mummy portraits from Fayum in this painting. See *Paula Modersohn-Becker zum Hundertsten Geburtstag,* cat. nos. 199, 388.

93   Folded Hands, 1898

List of Illustrations

Colour Plates

Cover: *Self Portrait with Hand on Chin*, 1906/7, oil on wood, 29 × 19.5 cm, Landesgalerie Hannover

I   *Self Portrait*, 1898, oil on board, 28.2 × 23 cm, Kunsthalle Bremen

II   *Nude Girl*, 1899, coloured chalk and charcoal, 136 × 68 cm, Graphisches Kabinett Wolfgang Werner KG, Bremen

III   *Self Portrait*, 1900, oil on board, 38 × 25.5 cm, Graphisches Kabinett Wolfgang Werner KG, Bremen

IV   *Girl with Flowers*, 1902/3, oil on wood, 47 × 33 cm, Staatliche Museen Preussischer Kulturbesitz, Nationalgalerie Berlin

V   *Girl and Boy*, 1903, oil on board, 54.5 × 36 cm, Ludwig-Roselius Sammlung, Böttcherstrasse, Bremen

VI   *Self Portrait*, 1903, oil on board, 38.5 × 25.5 cm, Kunsthalle Bremen

VII   *Evening Festival in Worpswede*, 1903, oil on board, 59 × 71.5 cm, Graphisches Kabinett Wolfgang Werner KG, Bremen

VIII   *Poorhouse Woman by the Duckpond*, 1904/5, oil on canvas, 42 × 62.5 cm, Ludwig-Roselius Sammlung, Böttcherstrasse, Bremen

IX   *Portrait of a Girl*, 1905, oil on canvas, 41 × 33 cm, Von der Heydt-Museum, Wuppertal

X   *Trumpeting Girl in the Birch Wood (Trumpeting Girl in the Woods)*, 1903/5, oil on canvas, 110.4 × 90.2 cm, Ludwig-Roselius Sammlung, Böttcherstrasse, Bremen

XI   *Old Woman with Headscarf*, 1904/5, oil on canvas, 35.3 × 35 cm, Ludwig-Roselius Sammlung, Böttcherstrasse, Bremen

XII   *Landscape with Houses, Birch Trees and Moon*, 1904/5, oil on board, 40.7 × 53.5 cm, Ludwig-Roselius Sammlung, Böttcherstrasse, Bremen

XIII   *Still Life: The Breakfast Table*, 1905, oil on board, 55 × 71.8 cm, Ludwig-Roselius Sammlung, Böttcherstrasse, Bremen

XIV   *Self Portrait on her Sixth Wedding Day*, 1906, oil on board, 101.5 × 70.2 cm, Ludwig-Roselius Sammlung, Böttcherstrasse, Bremen

XV   *Poorhouse Woman with a Glass Bowl*, 1906, oil on canvas, 96 × 80.2 cm, Ludwig-Roselius Sammlung, Böttcherstrasse, Bremen

XVI   *Rainer Maria Rilke*, 1906, oil on board, 32.3 × 25.4 cm,
         Ludwig-Roselius Sammlung, Böttcherstrasse, Bremen

XVII   *Girl with Stork*, 1906, oil on canvas, 73 × 59 cm, Private Collection

XVIII   *Reclining Mother and Child*, 1906, oil on canvas, 82 × 124.7 cm,
         Ludwig-Roselius Sammlung, Böttcherstrasse, Bremen

XIX   *Lee Hoetger*, 1906, oil on canvas, 92 × 73.5 cm, Ludwig-Roselius
         Sammlung, Böttcherstrasse, Bremen

XX   *Lee Hoetger*, 1906, oil on paper, 41 × 28 cm, Graphisches Kabinett
         Wolfgang Werner KG, Bremen

XXI   *Self Portrait with Amber Necklace*, 1906, oil on board, 62.2 × 48.2
         cm, Ludwig-Roselius Sammlung, Böttcherstrasse, Bremen

XXII   *Nude Girl with Flowers* (*Seated Nude Girl with Flowers*), 1907, oil on
         canvas, 89 × 109 cm, Von der Heydt-Museum, Wuppertal

XXIII   *Still Life with Tomatoes*, 1907, oil on canvas, 30 × 35 cm,
         Graphisches Kabinett Wolfgang Werner KG, Bremen

XXIV   *The Good Samaritan*, 1907, oil on paper, 31.2 × 37 cm,
         Ludwig-Roselius Sammlung, Böttcherstrasse, Bremen

XXV   *Kneeling Mother and Child*, 1907, oil on canvas, 113 × 74 cm,
         Ludwig-Roselius Sammlung, Böttcherstrasse, Bremen

Duotone Illustrations

1   *Self Portrait*, 1898/9, red chalk and charcoal, 27.1 × 22.6 cm,
     Graphisches Kabinett Wolfgang Werner KG, Bremen

2   *Woman on a Stool*, 1899/1900, charcoal, 59.5 × 28.3 cm,
     Ludwig-Roselius Sammlung, Böttcherstrasse, Bremen

3   *Standing Girl*, 1900/1906, charcoal and pastel, 61.3 × 29.4 cm,
     Ludwig-Roselius Sammlung, Böttcherstrasse, Bremen

4   *Girl in front of a Window*, 1902, oil on canvas, 49.3 × 49.5 cm,
     Private Collection

5   Otto Modersohn, *Autumn in the Moors*, 1895, oil on canvas,
     80 × 150 cm, Kunsthalle Bremen

6   Heinrich Vogeler, *Summer Evening at the Barkenhoff*, 1904-5,
     175 × 310 cm, Ludwig-Roselius Sammlung, Böttcherstrasse,
     Bremen

7   *Mother and Child*, 1898/9, charcoal and red chalk, 67 × 47.7 cm,
     Kunsthalle Bremen

8   *Worpswede Landscape*, 1900, oil on board, 61.5 × 67.8 cm,
     Wallraf-Richartz-Museum, Köln

9   Fritz Mackensen, *Prayers on the Moor*, 1895, oil on canvas,
     285 × 430 cm, Historisches Museum am Hohen Ufer, Hannover-
     Volkskundliche Abteilung

10 *Seated Girl*, 1898/9, black and red chalk, 49.4 × 36.2 cm,
Ludwig-Roselius Sammlung, Böttcherstrasse, Bremen

11 *Seated Male Nude*, 1898, charcoal and pencil, 68 × 41.7 cm,
Private Collection

12 *Spinning Peasant Woman*, 1899, charcoal, 80 × 54 cm, Private
Collection

13 *The Goosegirl*, 1899/1900, etching with aquatint, 25.1 × 20.3 cm

14 *Children with Geese*, 1900, black chalk, 29 × 40 cm, Private Collection

15 *Otto Modersohn Sleeping*, 1906, charcoal, 22.6 × 30.3 cm,
Kunsthalle Bremen

16 Otto Modersohn, *Paula Modersohn-Becker at Her Easel*, 1901, oil on
board, 58 × 41 cm, Private Collection

17 Heinrich Vogeler, *Spring*, 1898, oil on canvas, Haus im Schluh,
Worpswede

18 *Girl with Cat*, 1905, oil on canvas, 99 × 81.5 cm, Ludwig-Roselius
Sammlung, Böttcherstrasse, Bremen

19 *Teller of Fairytales*, 1900, oil on canvas, 51 × 69.5, Private Collection

20 *Self Portrait?*, 1897, charcoal, 34.5 × 27 cm, Kunsthalle Hamburg

21 *Standing Female Nude*, c1900, charcoal over pencil, Private Collection

22 *Standing Female Nude*, 1900, oil on canvas, 78.3 × 42.4 cm,
Kunsthalle Bremen

23 *Standing Male Nude*, 1896/7, charcoal, 62.1 × 41 cm, Private Collection

24 *Male Nude*, 1906, charcoal, 64 × 36.5 cm, Private Collection

25 *Head and Shoulders of a Woman*, 1898, charcoal, 48.3 × 62.5 cm,
Private Collection

26 *Standing Female Nude with Long Hair*, 1898, charcoal and red chalk,
65.6 × 40 cm, Private Collection

27 *Female Nude*, 1898, charcoal, 100 × 57.5 cm, Private Collection

28 *Standing Female Nude: Back View*, 1906?, charcoal, Private Collection

29 *Female Nude with Necklace*, 1906, charcoal, 31.5 × 11.7 cm,
Kunsthalle Bremen

30 *Two Female Nudes*, 1906, pencil, Kunsthalle Bremen

31 Lovis Corinth, *Reclining Nude*, 1896, oil on canvas, 75 × 120 cm,
Kunsthalle Bremen

32 *Reclining Nude*, 1905, oil on canvas, 70 × 112 cm, Private Collection

33 *Seated Female Nude*, 1906, charcoal, 56.8 × 33.2 cm, Kunsthalle
Bremen

34 *Figure Composition*, 1907, oil?, 110 × 74 cm, (now destroyed)

35 *Reclining Mother and Child*, 1906, charcoal, 22.9 × 31.2 cm,
Kunsthalle Bremen (See also Plate XVIII)

36 *Mother and Child*, 1903/4, charcoal, Private Collection

144

37 *Mother and Child*, 1907, oil on canvas, 80 × 59 cm, Museum am Ostwall, Dortmund

38 Fritz Mackensen, *Mother and Infant*, 1892, oil on canvas, 180 × 140 cm, Kunsthalle Bremen

39 *Peasant Woman and Child*, c1903, oil on canvas, 69 × 58 cm, Kunsthalle Hamburg

40 *Mother and Child*, 1906, oil on board, 105 × 75, Von der Heydt-Museum, Wuppertal

41 *Mother and Child*, oil on board, 74.5 × 52 cm, Von der Heydt-Museum ,Wuppertal

42 *Elsbeth*, 1902, oil on board, 89 × 71 cm, Ludwig-Roselius Sammlung, Böttcherstrasse, Bremen

43 Max Liebermann, *Eva*, 1883, oil on canvas, 95.3 × 67.2 cm, Kunsthalle Hamburg

44 *Portrait of a Sick Girl*, 1901, oil on canvas, 35 × 33 cm, Westfälisches Landesmuseum für Kunst und Kulturgeschichte, Münster

45 *Seated Girl*, 1899, charcoal, 60 × 42.9 cm, Ludwig-Roselius Sammlung, Böttcherstrasse, Bremen

46 *Young Girl with Yellow Flowers in Vase*, 1902, oil on board, 52 × 53 cm, Kunsthalle Bremen

47 *Infant with Mother's Hand,* 1903, oil on canvas, 31.3 × 26.7 cm, Kunsthalle Bremen

48 *Blind Little Sister*, 1905, oil on board, 32.2 × 33.5 cm, Wallraf-Richartz-Museum, Köln

49 *Nude Girl with Apple*, 1906, oil on canvas, 45.2 × 23 cm, Ludwig-Roselius Sammlung, Böttcherstrasse, Bremen

50 *Nude Boy*, 1906, charcoal, 31 × 23 cm, Private Collection

51 Ottilie Reyländer, *Sisters*, 1900, oil on canvas, Haus im Schluh, Worpswede

52 *Two Girls in a Landscape*, 1903/4, black chalk, 18.8 × 13.5 cm, Private Collection

53 *Design for 'Die Jugend'*, 1899, watercolour, 26.5 × 20.3 cm, Kunsthalle Bremen

54 *Design for 'La Ferme' Cigarettes*, 1900, watercolour and ink, 13.3 × 16.9 cm, Kunsthalle Bremen

55 *Girl with Pearl Necklace*, 1902, oil on board, 60.5 × 32 cm, Haus im Schluh, Worpswede

56 *Child with Goldfish Bowl*, 1906, oil on board, 105 × 46 cm, Haus der Kunst, München

57 *Seated Peasant Woman*, 1899, charcoal, 123 × 73 cm, Kunsthalle Kiel

58   *Peasant Girl Seated on a Chair*, 1905, oil on canvas, 90 × 61 cm, Kunsthalle Bremen

59   *Silent Mother*, 1903, oil on canvas, 70 × 58.8 cm, Landesgalerie Hannover

60   *Peasant Woman*, 1900, charcoal, 45.5 × 66 cm, Allan Frumkin Gallery, Chicago

61   *Seated Peasant*, 1899, charcoal, 123 × 73 cm, Kunsthalle Kiel

62   *Peasant with Cap*, 1899, black and red chalk, 74.9 × 40.9 cm, Ludwig-Roselius Sammlung, Böttcherstrasse, Bremen

63   *Peat Cutters*, 1900, oil on canvas, Haus am Weyerberg, Worpswede

64   *Peasant Woman with Red and Blue Headscarf*, 1905, oil on canvas, 35.3 × 35 cm, Haus am Weyerberg, Worpswede

65   *Sketch from the Tomb of Philippe Pot*, 1903, charcoal, 15 × 24 cm, Private Collection

66   *Old Woman with Handkerchief*, 1906, oil on board, 69 × 55 cm, Ludwig-Roselius Sammlung, Böttcherstrasse, Bremen

67   *Old Bredow*, 1899, black chalk, 70.1 × 45.4 cm, Ludwig-Roselius Sammlung, Böttcherstrasse, Bremen

68   Leopold von Kalckreuth, *The Old Woman*, 1894, Dresden Gemäldegalerie

69   *Old Peasant*, 1903, oil on canvas, 71 × 59 cm, Kunsthalle Hamburg

70   *Glade*, 1900, oil on board, 52.2 × 36.5 cm, Ludwig-Roselius Sammlung, Böttcherstrasse, Bremen

71   *Barn against an Evening Sky*, 1900, oil on board, 52 × 39 cm, Kunsthalle Bremen

72   *Boy with Grazing Goat*, 1902, oil on board, 50 × 70 cm, Von der Heydt-Museum, Wuppertal

73   *View from the Artist's Studio Window in Paris*, 1900, oil on canvas, 48.7 × 37.3 cm, Kunsthalle Bremen

74   *Still Life with Jug*, 1903, tempera on board, 51.5 × 49.5 cm, Kunsthalle Bremen

75   *Still Life with Blue and White Porcelain*, 1900, oil on board, 50 × 58 cm, Landesgalerie Hannover

76   *Still Life with Chestnuts*, 1905, oil on canvas, 65 × 90 cm, Von der Heydt-Museum, Wuppertal

77   *Still Life with Sunflower*, 1907, oil on canvas, 90 × 65 cm, Kunsthalle Bremen

78   *Still Life with Pumpkin*, 1905, oil on canvas, 75 × 95 cm, Von der Heydt-Museum, Wuppertal

79   *Still Life with Fruit*, 1905, oil on canvas, 67 × 84 cm, Kunsthalle Bremen

80 *Still Life with Apples and Green Glass*, 1906, oil on board, 33 × 42.7 cm, Ludwig-Roselius Sammlung, Böttcherstrasse, Bremen

81 *Still Life with Pottery Jug*, 1906, oil on canvas, 38 × 47 cm, Private Collection

82 *Sketch for Portrait of Clara Rilke-Westhoff*, 1905, charcoal, 27.3 × 18.7 cm, Kunsthalle Bremen

83 *Clara Rilke-Westhoff*, 1905, oil on canvas, 52 × 36.8 cm, Kunsthalle Hamburg

84 *Self Portrait*, 1903, coloured and black chalk, 22 × 20 cm, (whereabouts unknown)

85 *Woman with a Poppy*, 1900, oil on board, 57 × 46 cm, Ludwig-Roselius Sammlung, Böttcherstrasse, Bremen

86 *Herma*, 1906, oil on canvas, 55 × 47.2 cm, Worpsweder Archive

87 Clara Rilke-Westhoff, *Rainer Maria Rilke*, 1936, bronze portrait head, Kunsthalle Bremen

88 *Werner Sombart*, 1906, oil on canvas on plywood, 50 × 46 cm, Kunsthalle Bremen

89 *Young Woman with Red Hat*, 1900, oil on board, 68 × 45 cm, Kunsthalle Bremen

90 *Self Portrait with White Necklace*, 1906, oil on board, 41.5 × 26 cm, Westfälisches Landesmuseum für Kunst und Kulturgeschichte, Münster

91 *Self Portrait with Hand on Chin*, 1906, oil on canvas, 49 × 26.5 cm, Ludwig-Roselius Sammlung, Böttcherstrasse, Bremen

92 *Self Portrait with Camellia Branch*, 1907, oil on board, 62 × 30 cm, Museum Folkwang, Essen

93 *Folded Hands*, 1898, charcoal, 28.2 × 36.3 cm, Kunsthalle Bremen

Selected Bibliography

Augustiny, Waldemar, *Paula Modersohn-Becker,* Gütersloh, 1960
   Paula Modersohn, Hildesheim, 1971

Biermann, Georg, 'Paula Modersohn', *Junge Kunst,* Band 2, Berlin, 1927

Bremen, Graphisches Kabinett Wolfgang Werner KG, *Paula Modersohn-Becker,* 1971
   Graphisches Kabinett Wolfgang Werner KG, *Paula Modersohn-Becker, das Graphische Werk,* 1972

Bremen Kunsthalle, *Otto Modersohn,* 1965-6
   Kunsthalle, *Paula Modersohn-Becker zum Hundertsten Geburtstag* (G. Busch et al), 1976
   Kunsthalle, *Worpswede, Aus der Frühzeit der Künstlerkolonie,* 1970

Busch, Günter, *Paula Modersohn-Becker, Handzeichnungen,* Angelsachen, Bremen, 1949
   Paula Modersohn-Becker, Aus dem Skizzenbuch, Piper, Munich, 1960

Davidson, Martha, 'Paula Modersohn-Becker: Struggle between Life and Art'.
   The Feminist Art Journal, Winter, 1973-4

Faltus, Hermann, *Worpswede, Urteil und Vorurteil,* H. M. Hauschild, Bremen, 1972

Finke, Ulrich, *German Painting from Romanticism to Expressionism,* Thames and Hudson, London, 1974

Hamburg, Kunstverein, *Paula Modersohn-Becker: Zeichnungen, Pastelle, Bildentwürfe,* 1976

Heise, Carl Georg, *Die Sammlung des Freiherrn August von der Heydt,* Elberfeld/Leipzig, 1918
   Paula Becker-Modersohn: Mutter und Kind, Philipp, Stuttgart, 1961

Hetsch, Rolf (intro), *Paula Modersohn-Becker, Ein Buch der Freundschaft,* Rembrandt, Berlin, 1932. Reminiscences from Herma Weinberg, Otto Modersohn, Heinrich Vogeler, Ottilie Reyländer-Böhme, Fritz Mackensen, Clara Rilke-Westhoff, Rudolf Alexander Schröder, Rolf Hetsch, Helene Nostitz, Emil Waldmann, Hildegard Roselius, Maria Paschen, Albrecht Schaeffer and Manfred Hausmann

Langbehn, Julius, *Rembrandt als Erzieher,* Fritsch, Berlin, 1944

Modersohn-Becker, Paula, *Eine Kunstlerin, Paula Becker Modersohn, Briefe und Tagebuchblätter* (intro. S. D. Gallwitz), Hannover, 1917
Paula Modersohn-Becker, Briefe und Tagebuchblätter, List, Munich, 1957
Paula Modersohn-Becker, Briefe und Tagebuchblätter, S. Fischer Verlag, 1979

Murken-Altrogge, Christa, 'Der Französische Einfluss im Werk von Paula Modersohn-Becker', *Die Kunst,* March, 1975, pp. 145-52
Paula Modersohn-Becker, Kinderbildnisse, Piper, Munich, 1977

Murken-Altrogge, Christa, Murken, Axel Heinrich, 'Kinder, Kranke, Alte und Sieche: Symbole menschlicher Hinfälligkeit und Grösse. Medizinisches im Künstlerischen Werk von Paula Modersohn-Becker', *Deutsches Arzteblatt*, 71, 1974, pp. 1354-1359, 1433-1437

Nochlin, Linda, & Harris, Ann Sutherland, *Women Artists: 1550-1950,* Alfred A. Knopf, New York, 1976

Oppler, Ellen C., 'Paula Modersohn-Becker: Some Facts and Legends', *Art Journal* xxxv/4, 1976, pp. 364-369

Pauli, Gustav, *Paula Modersohn-Becker*, Leipzig, 1919. Third edition with expanded catalogue, Kurt Wolff, Berlin, 1934

Petersen, Karen, & Wilson, J. J, *Women Artists*, Harper and Row, New York, 1976; The Women's Press, London, 1978

Petzet, Heinrich Wiegand, *Das Bildnis des Dichters, Paula Modersohn-Becker und Rainer Maria Rilke*, Societäts, Frankfurt, 1957

Rilke, Rainer Maria, *Worpswede*, Velhagen & Klasing Bielefeld/Leipzig, 1903. Abridged edition, Schünemann, Bremen, 1970
Briefe aus den Jahren 1902-6, Leipzig, 1930

Seiler, Harald, *Paula Modersohn-Becker*, Munich, 1959

Selz, Peter, *German Expressionist Painting*, University of California Press, Berkeley, 1957,

Stelzer, Otto, *Paula Modersohn-Becker*, Rembrandt, Berlin, 1958

Vogeler, Heinrich, *Erinnerungen*, Rütten & Loening, Berlin, 1952

Werner, Alfred, 'Paula Modersohn-Becker: A Short Creative Life', *American Artist*, June, 1973, pp. 16-23, 68-70
'Paula Modersohn-Becker', *Art and Artists*, March, 1976